TABLE OF CONTENTS

WHAT KIND OF LIFE DO I WANT?

If someone had told me ten years ago that I would be writing a book about loss and life after loss, I never would have believed them. Profound loss was something that happened to other people. But a state of profound loss was exactly where I found myself in June of 2007 when my husband and best friend, Don, died suddenly in his sleep. He was only 54 years of age, and it was as peaceful a passing as any of us could ask for; but it was devastating to those of us left behind. And it changed EVERYTHING about my life.

I knew from grief support groups and books on grief and loss that not everyone experiences loss in such a dramatic way. Maybe the fact that I didn't have children of my own made the reversion to being "single" in every sense of the word more challenging because I didn't have the interaction with children and grandchildren to keep me busy. Maybe it was the fact that the timing of my husband's death resulted in a dramatic reduction of my financial resources which forced me to close my massage therapy practice. Maybe the fact that I didn't have an affiliation with a particular belief system left me floundering for answers. Maybe it was the fact that my husband was the one person in my life that seemed to truly "get" who I was and what I was about - and loved me in spite of it. Whatever the reasons, Don's sudden death left me emotionally devastated in a way that I did not think was possible.

I tried reconstructing my life. I tried creating a home for myself, resuming favorite activities, spending time with friends and family; and I even tried dating. All these things felt like I was playing "dress up". Because at my core I was empty (and not in the good Zen "all is emptiness" kind of way). It was as if there was nothing inside. There was no part of me that had anything to offer to anyone. Along with that came crushing and overwhelming feelings of anxiety. For me, the anxiety had mostly to do with money. How was I going to support myself? Would I have any money left for when I was "old"?

And then there was the anger.   For me it was more than anger; it was at times an all consuming sense of rage. Rage at my husband for dying so young, at the life insurance company that denied payment because he had died within the "contestability period"; rage at having to close my business, and jealousy at people who weren't going through what I was going through.   I felt rage toward the ones who were going through what I was going through and weren't all that pissed off about it.   When the rage wore off, there was just sadness, and then when the sadness wore off there was just the panic.   And then, when I got the panic under control with medication, there was just nothing. So rage, panic, and overwhelming sadness were my constant emotional companions; and after that just emptiness.   Not a good place in which to exist.

It took me nearly 4 years to reach that point of empty silence. But since nature abhors a vacuum, the silence turned into questions.   "Is this all there is?" "Is this what I'm left with"? "Is this what I am now"? These were not heartening questions. Because the only solution I had at the time to "fix" my problem was to get my old life back. Obviously, that wasn't an option.

With the help of a firm, but caring, counselor I came to the conclusion that I needed to change the way I was asking questions. So one evening sitting in bed and contemplating my empty life, I wrote down at the top of the page: "What Kind of Life Do I Want"?

One of the answers to that question was that living my life as I was, in that place of emptiness, was unacceptable. I knew that I needed to do something drastic to free myself from my current vicious cycle. After some brainstorming, I decided to sell my house, liquidate two thirds of my belongings, and go live in Bar Harbor, Maine (600 miles away) for at least a year. I had spent many happy vacations there; and in fact it was in nearby Acadia National Park that my late husband's ashes had been scattered. I knew the area, knew that there would be ample opportunity to hike, photograph, read, and hopefully begin true healing.   It was the fall of 2011, the housing market

was still in the pits, yet I was able to sell my house at full asking

price within two weeks.   I found a small studio apartment in Bar

Harbor, took a year-long lease, had a huge yard sale, and rented

a storage unit for the belongings that were left.   Within ten

weeks of making this decision, I was living in Maine.   And that is

when I began my real work.

I continued to ask myself the question "What Kind of

Life Do I Want?".   Moving to Maine was the first step, but it was

the other answers to that question and the things I did as a

result of those answers that were the genesis for this book.

Obviously, one of the answers was to bring writing back into my

life again, or we wouldn't be sitting here having this

conversation.   I knew that there had to be many more people

out there who had experienced a loss, not necessarily the loss

of spouse, but a loss of some kind that had left *them* feeling as

empty and hopeless as I did.

So who wants to read a book about feeling hopeless?!? Not many of you I presume. What follows are some essays where I will talk about those feelings of hopelessness, and discuss that place of emptiness. I share these essays for several reasons. First, if YOU are in that place, it is helpful to know that someone else is experiencing, or has experienced, the same or similar thoughts or feelings that you are. Second, it gives perspective on my journey; knowing where I started, the road I traveled, and where I am traveling now.

But most of these essays are about the journey itself. The observations, the "aha's", the shifts in thinking that helped me to emerge from that pit of despair and replace the emptiness with a sense of peace. I write it because I must. If it helps one other person struggling through a loss of hope, then it is worth the time it took to chronicle my journey.

WHAT IS LOSS and TELLING YOUR STORY

The loss that I refer to in writing these essays, is the about the sudden death of my husband, Don, at age 54. But loss comes in many shapes and forms. I think that any type of loss that changes your life in a significant way is going to be accompanied by feelings of grief. Aside from the death of someone close to you, here are some other examples.

- Loss of a home due to fire or natural disasters
- Accident or health crisis that alters your physical abilities, or those of someone close to you
- Loss of a job or a career or failure of business enterprise
- Wasting illness of someone close to you (such as dementia or Lou Gehrig's disease)
- Divorce or break up of a long- term relationship
- Prolonged estrangement from a child
- Significant change in financial status (often a secondary loss related to some other type of loss)

These are just a few examples of loss that will affect how you live your life on a daily basis.

Whatever type of loss you have suffered, you need to share your story. I don't mean you need (or even should) share every detail of your story with every person you meet. But you need to tell it often enough to help your mind process the reality of what has happened. When you say it out loud, or write it down, you are letting your mind know that it is real, that it is true. As time passes, you will have less need (or desire) to tell it; but you must trust me on this, and tell it you must.

So with that in mind, here is the story of my loss. It is June 29, 2007. Don is working 2nd shift at the company where he has worked for more than 30 years. He has only 2 months and 2 days until he is due to retire. I think he is as happy with his life as I have ever known him to be. He has stopped smoking, and though it is difficult, I know that he is thrilled that he has finally taken on his "monster". He is going to begin earnest study to become a certified personal trainer. He is very excited about this. Being 54 years old, he and I both believe that there is a market out there for middle aged folks who would like to work with a personal trainer closer to their own age, one who understands how different (and difficult) it is to get "in shape "at this point in your life versus when you are in your 20's or 30's. He wants me to be his first project!! :-)

He has become a grandfather twice (so far). Each of his two lovely daughters gave birth to their first child. One, a granddaughter, is 2 years old. The other, a grandson, has just been born. We have just returned from a visit to Tennessee to see his newest grandson. He is happy and proud that his children are doing so well. We also met his son's girlfriend and her parents. FINALLY, we think that Max (his son) is getting on track with his life. Max, a bright and truly likeable young man, has been a challenge. Neither disciplined nor goal oriented; he has drifted from job to job, always needing money, always searching. At this point in time, he still lives with his mother - but we think with his new girlfriend Karen, he is starting to really think about and plan for the future.

Thursday morning, June 29th, came as any other day. I woke stiff and sore from working a full schedule of massages the day before, and in a rather foul mood. I had several more clients scheduled for later that day. Don was back to work, after our vacation to Tennessee. Since he worked 2nd shift, our "together time" was always at the beginning of the day. I remember being grumpy as I started my day - watching the news. When Don got up we watched ESPN sports center, and me, grump, grump, grump through the whole morning. I remember apologizing to him before I left for my office about being in such a bad mood. As usual, he took it in stride. It was not a bother to him. Oh how I wish my mood had been so much different; and it would have been, had I known that was the last day I would spend with him alive.

I returned home from my office about the usual time, early evening; made my dinner and watched a little TV, all my normal evening activities. Don normally arrived home about

12:30 a.m., by which time I was fast asleep. This night was no different.   I woke at one point, thinking I heard him talking on the phone but drifted back to sleep. About 2 a.m. he came into the bedroom and turned on one of the lights. "What's wrong", I asked him. "Max got arrested tonight". My mind started racing - unable to imagine what his son could have possibly gotten arrested for. Don's disclosure was a complete and total shocker, for the charge was a serious one. Max was 24 and engaged to be married the following summer. By this point Don had only spoken with his ex- wife, Max's mother, and his two daughters. Other than the charge, of which we had few details, the only other thing he really knew was that Max was going to be arraigned early in the morning when bail would be set. Don climbed into bed - he was very quiet.   "What are you thinking, what are you feeling?" I asked him. "I'm thinking about how I'm going to get to Tennessee, and wondering what the bail will be". "Where are we going to get the money for that?" I said quietly. As money manager of the house, it was I who knew what money was where; and I was concerned that the only place we would be able to get any real money would be from one of our retirement accounts. Not a pleasant prospect. I asked Don: "Are you feeling okay?", because he continued to be very quiet. Knowing him, he was probably somehow blaming himself for Max's screw up; because that is how my husband was.

Don tells me he's having a little trouble breathing, but he thinks it is just his asthma acting up from the stress. I asked him if he wanted me to heat up one of our herbal packs that we used almost daily for aches and pains, for breathing, and for relaxation. He said yes, so I got up and threw one into the microwave. While my husband's reaction was one of shock, disbelief, self blame, and "I love my kid"; I on the other hand was starting to feel angry. Angry that Max had been so stupid, so selfish, and about to need money from us (once again).

When the microwave finished warming up the herbal pack, I returned to bedroom and put it on Don's chest. I also started to massage his shoulders and abdomen. I asked him again, "Are you okay?", and he said that he was feeling better. The last thing I told him before he went to sleep was "I love you". He said "I know you do. I love you too." He fell asleep holding my hand.

Of course by this time I was working up a good head of steam, and was wide awake. I got up and went to the office, jumped on-line and began researching the penalties for the charges filed against Max. I searched for some lawyers in the Knoxville area. I ran budget numbers. I stewed and brewed. Finally, at around 4:30 a.m. I fell asleep on the sofa. It was a restless sleep and during this period I had what I can only describe as a "waking dream". In the dream I was on my cell phone talking to Pat (Don's ex wife), and I was saying "I have bigger problems to deal with than Max getting arrested because during the night Don died". I call it a "waking dream" because I was aware of saying this, and thinking I should wake up, but I could not wake up.

I actually did wake up about 8:30 a.m., and the

bedroom door was closed, as I had left it a few hours before. It wasn't unusual for Don to sleep until 9:30 a.m. or so, after working 2nd shift. Considering what was going on I knew he had to be exhausted. It never occurred to me to check on him, because it was not out of the ordinary for him to be asleep at this hour.

I fixed some tea, then went into my office to make a few business related phone calls, spent some time on the computer, and did paperwork. By 10:30 a.m. Don still was not up and he was scheduled to work that day, Friday; although I knew he would likely take off to deal with the Max problem. I thought I had better wake him, as I knew the day ahead would be a busy one.

As soon as I opened the bedroom door, I knew he was dead. Of course I hadn't really internalized it yet, but my brain knew. He had a strange gray pallor to him. Other than that, he looked like he was sleeping; lying on his left side with his left hand tucked under his cheek. His eyes were closed. I rushed to the bed and touched him, he was cold. I screamed "no Don, oh no Don, no, No, NO", and recoiled backing into the closet doors. Then I touched him again, and started shaking him, all the while screaming - no, no, no.   Tears were streaming down my face. I was shaking all over.   I ran to get my phone (all we used were cell phones - we had no landlines).   I could not remember how to dial 911. I think I was dialing the number, but not hitting send.   After several attempts, I called my mother, since they only lived 7 miles away. I was hysterical - I was crying "Don is dead, Don is dead, I can't call 911 - please call them".   After I finished that call I went back into the bedroom, shook him some more and got even more hysterical.   I went next door to my neighbor since I knew she was home during the day. I remember sagging to the floor after she answered the door, and telling her what had happened.

I should pause here to talk about my general temperament. I am considered by myself and others to be a logical, problem-solving kind of person. I am not highly emotional – it is (was) rare for me to cry, or have extremes of any emotion. I pride myself on remaining calm under pressure. The shock of finding my husband dead, in an instant, changed my emotional profile for months and years to come.

By this point, my neighbor had gone into our bedroom to see for herself that Don was dead; and came back and called 911. They, of course, had already received the call from my mother and indicated that someone was on the way. We lived in a secured building, so my neighbor went downstairs to wait for the police and/or ambulance while I returned to sit shell shocked on the bed next to Don.

As surreal as finding him dead was, things got even more surreal when the police arrived. Due to his age, and the fact that he had no previous medical history of heart problems, the police had to question me. Two different officers questioned me at separate times - I assume to see if my story stayed consistent. They looked through our medicine cabinet, and checked Don's cell phone and mine for incoming and outgoing phone calls. I, of course, gave the back story about Don's son and his difficulty with breathing before he went to sleep. They told me they had to have the coroner come to inspect the body before a funeral home could take his body. The coroner concluded that it was either an undiagnosed heart condition or an aneurism that had burst in the brain.

During all this questioning my parents arrived, and of course, Don's cell phone was ringing and ringing with calls from Don's ex-wife, Max's mother. My "waking dream" was about to come true.

I have contemplated many times in the months and years since Don's death about that" waking dream" – wondered if I would have woken up and checked on Don if I could have saved him, as though the dream were some kind of warning. I wondered if I had in fact "fast forwarded" through time, and what I was viewing in my "waking dream" was the future. I wondered if I was having that dream at the very instant he died.

Telling Don's ex-wife was bad enough. Telling his

oldest daughter Kara who also lived in Tennessee, was the hardest phone call I have ever had to make in my life. If any of you reading this have had to make a phone call of this type, you understand what I am saying. How do you tell a beautiful, sensitive, new mother of 26 years of age (who already had the shock of hearing her brother was arrested), that her beloved father was dead? Don's ex- wife told his son in the prison, along with the prison chaplain. His other daughter was told by her fiancé, so I was spared having to make three horrible phone calls. Of course his employer had to be called, appointments had to be cancelled; and the rest of Don's family, as well as my own, had to be notified.

Grief books talk about the protective shock that settles in after a tragedy of this nature. I would have to say that is true - the mind goes into a state of detachment, and becomes more of an observer than a participant. Part of your mind recognizes that, yes, this is all happening to you; but another part of the mind looks upon the activities, conversations, and actions as though they were happening to someone else.   I will say this. I believe that on that day part of my mind shattered or short circuited. Oh, I have no conclusive tests to prove it; and my sister would have me blame it on menopause.   But my ability to concentrate, to remember detailed instructions, to remember names, places, and events has never returned to what it was prior to that day.   It is as if some brain cells, some connections, were permanently "fried".   If, and when, those abilities will return to their "pre- death" levels remains to be seen.

That is MY story, and each of you reading this has your own. You need to tell it, you need to talk about it; you may even need to write it down. My loss is no greater or smaller than the one you are experiencing. While it is good to keep perspective, and realizing that "it can always be worse"; it is still important that you acknowledge your loss and the feelings of grief associated with it for what it is. Ignoring those feelings, minimizing them, denying them will only prolong the healing process.

I tell you my story now so that you can use it for context in reading the other essays in this book. May it help you to be fearless in telling your own story, and in processing your grief.

Author's note: Some names in this essay have been changed

PRE HIKE INSTRUCTIONS – A METAPHOR FOR GRIEVING

When I first arrived in Maine it was late November, just after Thanksgiving. The winter I spent there was a mild one, from a snow standpoint, and even from a cold standpoint, as we would get a bitterly cold day here and there, but no prolonged cold spells. This meant that I was able to get outside and hike in Acadia National Park, which I fondly referred to as my backyard. Within ten minutes from the small, studio apartment I rented in the town of Bar Harbor, I could be hiking along the ocean, or a lake, or up a mountain. The variety was tremendous.

One of the things that make Acadia National Park special is the system of "Carriage Roads" that wind through and around some of the most scenic areas. The roads were designed and built by John D Rockefeller Jr., who later became the single largest benefactor of Acadia National Park, donating large parcels of land that included his wonderful Carriage Roads.

These carriage roads are strictly for non vehicular traffic. Bikers, hikers, joggers and horseback riders are able to use these roads throughout the year.   Due to the lack of snowfall, I was able to use these roads for hiking until mid January when they did become covered with a thick coat of ice.   Many trails begin and end at some point along the carriage roads which is why the following sign appears at the entrance point to the roads:

- You are entering back country

- Take plenty of water

- Tell someone your plans

- Darkness falls early in winter, plan your trip

- Stay on the trail

- Cairns are there to guide hikers, do not remove or alter cairns

- Look for and follow the blue blaze

As I hiked that day I thought about how after a loss such as the one I had suffered,   to effectively deal with that loss, I needed to have a set of "instructions" if you will - coping

strategies and ways to manage the hours, days, and weeks that

would follow. I think this metaphor is especially appropriate to

getting through the shock of the early days of grieving.

"You are entering back country" - Indeed the term "back

country" aptly describes the unfamiliar landscape of grief and

loss. Everything looks different. Everything feels strange. We

are bewildered, confused, and uncertain about where we are,

how we got there, and how to find our way out. In the first few

weeks after Don's death I could not conceive how the world was

just continuing along its merry way. I was "a stranger in a

strange land", because for me time had stopped. I was indeed

taking a trip into a place that I had no idea how to navigate

through, and my ability to survive seemed unlikely.

"Take plenty of water" – You're gonna need it, just to keep

yourself hydrated from all the crying! Water is essential to

survival for the hiker because if he or she becomes dehydrated,

weakness and confusion can set in and the hiker may not be

able to safely return. From a grief management standpoint, I encourage you to be totally and completely selfish while you are grieving, especially initially. You need to focus on your own survival – get as much rest as you can, eat healthy foods, and do drink plenty of water.   If the people around you can't deal with you being a little selfish, then surround yourself with different people.   It doesn't mean that you are going to be selfish forever, but you have just survived a shock – it is no different than if you had major surgery or were injured in a car accident. You must take care of yourself and conserve your emotional and physical strength if you are to get through this first stage of grief.

"Tell someone your plans" – Hikers, especially if they are hiking alone, are encouraged to let someone know where they are going, and when they expect to return.   When it comes to grieving and loss, you are going to need support – no one, I repeat NO ONE can get through this alone. Different people will play different roles for you during these first days and weeks. Some will be emotionally supportive, some will bring you food, some will provide distractions, some will clean your house or mow your yard, some will call you or email you each day to see how you are, and quite frankly, some will disappear. Don't be surprised or angered by this – realize that some people simply cannot cope with the strong emotion you are dealing with.   Also, some people are so terrified by the prospect of death that they will turn away and risk losing you as a friend because this is easier for them then the prospect of confronting that which they fear so deeply.   Let them go.   In time some of them may come back to you. You can decide at that time if you want to bring them back into your life and if so in what role. Not everyone is capable or qualified to bear this responsibility. It will add to your hurt when you first realize this about them, but don't waste time or emotional energy on it. You need all your strength to survive.

"Darkness falls early in winter – plan your trip" - The sooner you realize and accept your limitations while you are grieving, the better off you will be.   You are going to need more sleep

than usual.   You are going to feel drained and exhausted.   You

are going to have unpredictable mood swings.   To the extent

that you are able, take time off from work.   Find help caring for

children or elderly parents (if these things are included among

your responsibilities).   An argument can be made for "keeping

busy" after a loss; and I am sure that for some people this helps

them to cope.   In my opinion, this just delays dealing with the

inevitable.   You need to feel what you need to feel; and better

to do so now than have it jump up and smack you in the face

several months or years from now.

"Stay on the trail" – Grieving is less of a process, and more like

a journey.   Experience it, but don't lose yourself.   Don't give

into using alcohol, drugs, food, sex, or other negative

distractions thinking it will just be a temporary thing to help you

get by.   Temporary "things" soon become habits, and habits

can become addictions.   You've got enough to deal with in the loss you have suffered.   Don't make it harder by complicating your life with vices.

"Cairns are there to guide hikers, do not move or alter Cairns" – By way of follow up to the last paragraph, DO seek out the help of professionals.   Hospice centers around the country do a wonderful job of running grief support groups for a death loss of all types (it doesn't have to be from an illness).   From one on one counseling, to support groups (made up of other survivors like you); to lending libraries (filled with all sorts of books, DVDs, and videos on grieving) they are there to support you in this journey.   Likewise, if your insurance plan includes a mental health component, seek out a counselor who has experience in grief counseling (you may have to try several until you find a "match").   If you are religiously inclined, your faith based organization may offer support groups and/or counseling. While I don't recommend drugs like alcohol, marijuana or cocaine to help get you by – if you are having trouble sleeping, experiencing extreme anxiety or depression – work with a medical professional you trust and use some prescription medicine.   Seek out alternative health providers such as acupuncturists, massage therapists, and yoga instructors. There are many professionals out there who have studied and worked hard to prepare themselves to help people in times of deep suffering.   They are there to help you.   Look for them.

"Look for and follow the blue blaze" – For the non- hikers out there, the blue blaze are markings made along the trail with bright blue paint.   Often painted on tree trunks or on rocks (when there are no trees) they are there to help the hiker identify the direction of the trail. I liken the blue blaze to intuition.   That small voice within us that tells us how we are really feeling, at what level we are suffering, and what we need to do to help ourselves.   Listen to this voice.   Give yourself time to be quiet. Give yourself time to be alone (scary at first, but oh so worth it).   Sit with your voice. Write down what you are hearing.   There will be times when all you hear is weeping, so weep.   There will be times when all you hear is anger, so be angry. There will be times when you hear laughter, so laugh.

Let the voice tell you if it needs some professional help (which I

STRONGLY recommend). Let the voice tell you if you are

drinking too much (then do something about it). Let the voice

tell you if you need more time alone, or need more time with

others.   If you can learn to listen to your inner "blue blaze", the

path will become clear and you will find your way home.

YOU CAN'T FIGHT THE WIND

I moved to Maine Thanksgiving weekend. Half of the people I know told me I must be crazy to be moving to Maine at the start of winter. The other half probably *thought* I was crazy, but were too polite to say so. I knew that Maine winters tended to be long, dark, cold, and snowy. My new landlords had told me that the two previous winters had seen especially heavy snowfall. January usually brought bitter cold that could last a few days or a few weeks. What they didn't tell me about was the wind.

That winter in Maine ended up being unusually mild. Temperatures warmed just as winter storms neared the coast, giving us rain instead of snow. Hard freezes came, but were quickly followed by thaws. Cold spells lasted a day or two then broke. But the wind was almost constant. It came from any and all directions depending on weather systems that seemed to collide over Mount Desert Island. I came to learn that anything less than 25mph was considered "breezy" and high wind warnings weren't issued until sustained winds exceeded 35mph.

A lack of snowfall, which in Pennsylvania (where I grew up) is reason for (most) people to rejoice, is lamented by Mainers.   One of the things I came to appreciate about living on Mount Dessert Island is that most people here really enjoy being physically active.   Back at work on Monday mornings conversations tended to center on where they had been hiking, biking, or camping, rather than on where they had shopped, eaten, or what movies they watched.   This is true even during the winter months when cross country skiing, ice skating, snowmobiling, and ice fishing are favorite pastimes.   The lack of snow and prolonged cold spells gave little opportunity for these pastimes. It did, however, mean that many hiking trails remained passable, especially in the meadows and valleys. Bikers enjoyed the park loop road in Acadia National Park every month except January, when a thick layer of ice covered all hard surfaces.

Wind was just another fabric that made up the quilt of island life.   Fashion was eschewed in favor of practicality. Two solid investments were a quality pair of boots and a jacket (I think it is no coincidence that LLBean began in Maine).   If you are going to live year-round along the coast of Maine, you learn to accept and adapt to whatever Mother Nature brings. Umbrellas are pointless, because whenever it rains, the wind comes with it.   A much better investment is a long raincoat with a secure hood.

As time passed, I learned to work with the wind. I learned that when the wind blew out of the northwest, the coastal mountains protected the shore path that ran along the ocean making hiking there in the winter sunshine a temperate (and usually private) pleasure. When the wind blew in off the ocean, you could retreat to the protected stretches of paths in the woods behind the meadow. When it really got to swirling and howling, you quickly accomplished your walking errands in town and then caught up on your reading.

The wind in Maine is a lot like loss.   It is always there. You are never sure from which direction it is coming until you get outside. It can be a cold, bone chilling wind, or a mild warm breeze. You learn that sometimes loss is like that bone chilling kind of wind; cold and harsh, reminding of you what you have lost. You learn that sometimes loss is like that warm breeze; a fond memory of good times. You learn that sometimes loss is like the howling wind; it is best to do what you need to do and then retreat until it passes.

You can't fight the wind anymore than you can fight a loss. You can only accept that it is there and make the best of it. You adapt and figure out ways of coping that make it easier to tolerate. You respect it, but you don't let it keep you from going outside to enjoy the sunshine, breathe the fresh air, or appreciate the scenery. You realize that sometimes the wind brings in the storms, but sometimes it blows them away. You realize that the wind is a part of life and that it affects everyone sooner or later. You can try and fight it, but it would be like using an umbrella in a Maine coast rainstorm, frustrating and pointless. Better to put on the long trench coat, pull up the hood and go jump in the puddles.

Wind is a force of nature. It doesn't pick and choose where it blows or how hard. It's the same with loss. So stop fighting.

THE CATS THAT SAVED MY LIFE

Let me introduce you to my two cats. Pebbles and Bam Bam both came to live with Don and I as strays. Their personalities are as different as night and day. Pebbles, the female, tends to be a one person cat (me), a loner, window watcher, fairly low maintenance in the attention department. Bam Bam, the male is much more social, very emotionally needy and wants to be where ever his humans are at all times. Pebbles had been living in our garden for five months until in November it got cold and we invited her to come inside. Eventually she did, becoming a fulltime member of our household. The next summer Bam Bam showed up at our back door. When Don opened the door, Bam Bam walked in, laid down, and when he rolled over to have his belly rubbed, he instantly became a member of the family. Pebbles is a calico with beautiful white markings. Bam Bam is coal black without a single spot of any other color on him.

If you have pets and someone tries to tell you that animals don't grieve, don't believe them. When Don died, Bam Bam would get up every night around the time that Don got home from work. Bam Bam would wander the condo meowing. This went on for about four months. I put one of Don's old jackets on Bam Bam's favorite sleeping pillow and that seemed to soothe him. Pebbles, who's only use for Don was the cheese that he fed her, did not seem to miss him, but she was highly sensitive to my moods   (which for the first 6 - 9 months bordered on insanity) and it caused her so much stress that she ended up getting sick.

People have asked me to describe grief. I can tell you what it is for me, and that it is different for everyone. I can tell you also what it is *not*. It is not the nice, neat "five stages of grief" that gets bantered about in our society -- Denial, Anger, Bargaining, Depression, and Acceptance; which, oh by the way, should take about 12 – 18 months to process for a major loss. The reality is that grief isn't anywhere near that neat and tidy.

As with anything else that is difficult and ugly, our society tries to sanitize it, give it a process, a system that if those of us going through it would just follow, things will be back "to normal" in no time, and we can all get on with our lives. If you are grieving and someone tries to tell you that "this is the way it should be", you have my permission to tell them to go fuck themselves.

This is especially true in the early days. For me numbness and shock lasted about a week. After that it was like being thrown into a deep, dark well filled with dirty stinking water. It was overwhelming, it was all consuming. It was hurling things against the walls and screaming at the tops of my lungs. It was crawling into one of the corners of my condo which I termed my "weeping corners", and curling myself into as small a ball as possible and sobbing for hours at a time. It was going to sleep and hoping that I didn't wake up. It was the "I cannot continue to live" kind of grief.

I considered suicide. It seemed, at the time, a totally viable option. Anything that would give me relief from the burning, searing pain of loss that I was feeling was worth considering. No matter that it was a permanent solution. Don had left me quickly and without warning; how could he (or anyone else) expect me to go on and function as a normal human being? It may bear mentioning that I have never (prior to this loss) been clinically depressed. I considered myself pretty resilient. It was a rude awakening to learn that I was just as vulnerable, and just as out of control as the rest of humanity when tragedy strikes.

My plan for ending it all was a good plan, not too messy. Our condo, being in a restored factory, had 20 foot high ceilings with large wooden beams. Those beams were perfect to hang yourself from. I had it all worked out. I'd get the large community ladder into the condo (because you have to climb up there somehow). I checked out different types of rope at the hardware store, and read up on- line about knot tying. I would sit on the floor of the condo and look up at those beams picturing how it would be, analyzing my plan for flaws. There were three that I identified:

1. I felt really bad for the person or persons who would get
   stuck finding me.

2. Having no experience with this sort of thing, I was
   concerned that I'd screw it up and either end up in a
   mental institution or with brain damage.

   And.......

3. What would become of my cats?

That last one really got me thinking. What would happen
to my cats?! While there were plenty of cat lovers in my family,
they all had animals of their own. My sister and her husband
might have taken them, but at the time they were often
traveling. My cats weren't used to being around children
and/or other animals, so adjusting to completely new
circumstances would have been very hard on them. Being
middle aged cats (7 and 8 respectively), they would have been
harder to adopt out. Plus, after all they had already been

through with the loss of one of their humans, and left with another insane and unpredictable one, was it really fair to put them through more? After all, didn't taking in an animal mean that you were giving them a "forever home"? To think of them being put down because a home couldn't be found for them - well that to me was even more tragic a thought than that of taking my own life.

So, at the beginning of my grief journey when I wanted to end it all, it was two furballs that gave me a reason to get up in the morning - because even if I didn't care if I got out of bed, or if I lived or died - they wanted to eat, they wanted fresh litter, they wanted my attention and affection. They were *my* cats and *my* responsibility. When you're hanging by a thread (so to speak), it doesn't really matter what it is that keeps you from climbing that ladder, or taking those pills, or pulling that trigger - what matters is that you find SOMETHING that keeps you here in this world, even if it's just a couple of cats.

The good news is that I did find a way to climb out of that

deep, dark well. It wasn't pretty and it wasn't painless. I made some bad decisions on the way out. And it certainly wasn't "Five stage/Keibler Ross" orderly, as I careened from one "stage" to the other, back and forth; making progress, slipping backwards; one step forward, two steps back. You and I, we didn't choose this blackness of grief; but you are going to get out of bed, and you are going to put one foot in front of the other. You will act like you are making progress, when inside you are a broken, empty vessel. You will remind yourself that you have responsibilities that someone or something *is* depending on you. You are going to feel terrible, but you *are* going to get better; so grab your lifelines and hang on to them with every remaining ounce of strength that you have. *No one* is going to feel *exactly* what you feel while you are grieving. Even though my experience is not the same as yours, I am living proof that you *can* survive this. Hold on.

EVERYTHING CHANGES

Shortly after moving to Bar Harbor I began taking a yoga class. It was a good way to meet some new people, to get out of the house on those cold, dark evenings, and a good way to unwind my tense body. The class I took was called "Foundations of Yoga". It was deemed a beginners class because the instructor concentrated on teaching the fundamentals of each pose. In addition, I learned that my instructor had recently been ordained as a Zen Buddhist priest. This was NOT something I had expected to find in Bar Harbor, but nevertheless was intrigued to learn of her journey and looked forward to participating in her class.

At one of my classes I found myself in a pose that involved standing on one foot with the other leg stretched out, one arm bracing me (on a yoga block) and the other arm extended in the air, a pose that I actually managed to achieve and hold for a few seconds! From this pose we went back to a simple "mountain pose", which is just standing, both feet straight ahead, arms at your sides. Our instructor remarked very quietly when we had returned to mountain pose: *"just think, a few seconds ago you were standing on one leg with one arm in the air and now here you are with both feet on the ground. Everything changes, everything changes".*

Everything changes. That simple phrase hit me like a freight train. I've read and researched so many philosophies that talk about how the only thing certain in life is change, or that change is the only constant in the universe - but somehow connecting this concept to the action of the yoga poses drove it home to me in a way that I had not previously internalized. *Everything changes.*

Everything changes. One day you are a child living with your parents, the next you are married with a home of your own. One moment you are a couple, the next moment you are a parent. One moment your parents are youthful, vibrant people, the next your father doesn't know what day it is because of dementia. One moment you are married to a wonderful man, the next day he is dead and you are a widow. One moment you have a successful business, the next you are scrambling to find a job and make ends meet. One moment you are living in Pennsylvania, the next you are in Bar Harbor, Maine and writing a blog. *Everything changes.*

Everything changes. Every moment of every day, something is changing. The cells in your body, the clouds overhead, the smell in the air, the view before you, the people

47

around you. Some changes are large, some are small. Some changes have positive outcomes, others negative. Inevitably change is there staring us in the face......*everything changes.*

Everything changes. We are not alone in this universe of change. Just as "our" world is changing, so is the world of every other living thing changing. Our family, our friends, our stranger on the street, our pets, our plants, our ocean, our desert, our planet. Every living thing needs to react and adapt to these changes - be they subtle or not so subtle.

Everything changes. Each one of us reacts to change in different ways. In the past my response was to try and control the change occurring around me. An impossible task, but still I tried. Of course now I realize that these attempts were a valiant if ineffective effort to cope. I would also label change - good/bad, positive/negative, large/small, manageable/unmanageable.

In reality change is none of these things; it is what it is - just change, just things being different than they were before. The labels we apply to change, our reaction to it, our <u>resistance</u> to it is where our suffering begins. The more we resist, the more we try to control, the more we label, the more we suffer. Understanding this basic concept is simple, accepting it is not as simple.   Once it is grasped and accepted we can open ourselves up to experiencing change in a whole new way. We can look at it with appreciation, rather than fear or dread. When I feel the anxiety about the change occurring in my life, I stop whatever I'm doing for a few minutes, take a deep breath and remind myself that what is happening is normal, it is not just a phenomena happening to me, but that changes are happening EVERYWHERE. This change will not last forever, it will be replaced by another change, and then another, and another, and so on. And since whatever change I am experiencing at that moment is not going to last, why label it? That old saying from the 1970(s) (or was it the 80's) "Go With the Flow" comes to mind. It sounds corny, but really it sums up beautifully how we can approach change with an open mind and an open heart.

Remember - Everything Changes.

A FEW WORDS ON BRAVERY

Definitions:

Brave – to face or endure with courage

Courage – the mental or moral strength to venture, persevere, and withstand danger, fear, or difficulty.

Before I moved to Maine, I shared with family and friends my reasons for wanting to make that change. A few of them, I'm sure, thought I was having a mental breakdown (but were kind enough not to say so), some thought I was being selfish and/or reckless (including myself from time to time), but nearly everyone was supportive. A few of them even told me how much they admired my "courage". Once I got to Maine and I met new people they would ask me what had brought me there.   I would briefly share my story saying something like: "I have vacationed here for years and always wondered what it would be like to live here year-round (true). A few years ago my husband passed away, and I've been rather at loose ends ever since. I thought a change in scenery would be a good way

50

to blast myself out the rut I felt I was getting into". Nine times out of ten I would get a response from them that included the word "brave".

While I appreciated the words of encouragement and support from family and friends (old and new), I personally had difficulty identifying with words like "brave" and "courageous" when applied to myself and my situation.   Brave and courageous were two of last things I had felt since Don's death. Most of the time I used words like "fearful, anxious, angry, frustrated, stuck, depressed, sad, lonely, empty, and resentful". Although I felt that the decision to relocate to Maine was the right one at the right time, the words "necessary and survival" seemed more appropriate than "brave or courageous".

By this point in time it had been more than four years since Don had died.   Far from feeling brave about the whole thing, I was in fact completely frustrated with what I perceived as a failure to recover from this loss.   After all, I was known for my ability to problem solve, for my ability to "move on" after disappointment, and my ability to adapt to new and different situations.   But this was different. And I had two schools of thought about where I was at mentally and emotionally.   Either I was a complete failure at managing this change that had been thrust upon me, or I had gotten very, very good at identifying myself with this loss – sort of a professional griever.   Neither of these definitions of my status involved being brave or courageous!

So I was puzzled by the idea that so many people felt that what I was doing was "brave".   In my mind, bravery was reserved for people risking their lives for another, or someone enduring torture and confinement.   People who stood up and spoke truth while others buried their heads in the sand were brave. People like Mahatma Ghandi, Nelson Mandela, and Jackie Kennedy.

Is bravery a large act or a small one? Can bravery and courage be something as simple as getting out of bed?   Can it be as small as going to a dinner party as a newly single person?

Can it be that we are much more demanding of ourselves then others are of us, and therefore overlook our own acts of courage?   Is bravery overcoming fear, or is it the acknowledgment of fear and pressing forward in spite of it?

I'd like to be able to look in the mirror and see brave. I'd like to wake up each morning and think courage.   I'm not there yet.   I'm still operating in the mode of doing what I feel I need to do in order to have the kind of life that I want.   Some of those steps are riskier than others.   Is that courage? Maybe.   Am I being brave or foolish?   It's a fine line. If there is ANYTHING that Don's sudden death taught me, is that life can change in a heartbeat (literally).   Now that I know that, I'm much less keen to sit around and hope that my situation will change or hope that things will get better.   I realize that "time is NOT always on my side", and that waiting until tomorrow can be too late.

Maybe being brave is as simple as just getting up in the morning.   Maybe being brave is as small as forcing ourselves to get out of the house and take a walk when all we really feel like doing is escaping with a book, or TV, drinking wine, or eating nachos.   Maybe courage is looking in the mirror and telling yourself that you ARE going to survive this.   Maybe courage is looking for beauty and practicing gratitude in the midst of anguish and heartache.   Step by step we practice courage by simply surviving.   As we get stronger we take greater risks, we allow ourselves to venture back into the land of the living; and before you know it, people are calling us "brave".

"DUKKAH" HAPPENS

During my journey I came to find that many of the principles unique to Buddhism, and Zen Buddhism in particular held great wisdom for me and helped me to better understand and cope with my loss. The first of these is the concept of "Dukkah".

In Buddhism, regardless of which "school" of thought you subscribe to, there are "The Four Noble Truths". The wording changes depending on the translation and interpretation, but the essence remains. The Four Noble Truths are:

1. Life means suffering

2. Suffering is caused by attachment

3. There is a way to end suffering

4. Following "the path" results in the cessation of suffering

I want to share with you *my* understanding of the first and second of these four noble truths. I don't claim to be a Buddhist, and you certainly don't have to become a Buddhist to apply these principles when dealing with loss and/or living your life.

The word "suffering" is often used when translating the word "dukkah". A better translation of dukkah is "to experience unease or discomfort". But in order to make this concept easier for us westerners to understand, the word suffering is used. For those of you who may not know the Buddha's story; he was born and raised as a prince. His parents did everything possible to make sure that he was never exposed to anything unpleasant, so he grew up in an opulent, beautiful world, leading a charmed existence. It was not until he was a young man that he rebelled (as most young men do), and insisted on being driven outside of the palace walls. There he was exposed to poverty, sickness, and death. He realized that there was a whole other side to life that he knew nothing about.

In his desire to understand the suffering that he saw he chose to forsake his comfortable life at the palace and pursue what he termed "enlightenment".

We all suffer.   Human nature is not perfect and neither is the world we live in. Everyone experiences unease and discomfort. During our lifetime, we will endure physical suffering such as pain, sickness, injury, tiredness, old age (if we are lucky), and death.   We will also endure psychological suffering like sadness, fear, frustration, grief, anger and disappointment.   Suffering comes in different shapes and sizes, but it comes to everyone. So do positive experiences, which we view as the opposite of suffering.   Of course we all strive to spend as much of our lives as possible dwelling in the realm of these positive experiences. This is an unrealistic expectation, so when our times of "unease and discomfort" come as they do, we experience suffering.

I have come to believe that we experience suffering because we don't want to accept that *all things are impermanent.*   On the surface, we all say "well of course, I know that", thus the adage "nothing lasts forever". But do we *really, truly* grasp this?   Of course some things are more permanent than others. For example the granite rocks that make up the mountains of my beloved Acadia National Park have been there for thousands, if not hundreds of thousands of years. But they will disappear with time and reappear in another form. Lightening bugs on the other hand have a very short life expectancy, so they are much more impermanent than the granite. But everything is impermanent. This includes our emotions.   Think about what you consider to have been the happiest day of your life. It may be the day you got married, or the day your child was born.   You were euphoric. You anticipated and looked forward to the joy you knew you were going to feel at this event.   Did those feelings last? Of course not. You find out that your partner has annoying habits when you live with them 24/7, and that having a baby is exhausting; not all sweet smells and cuddles. Impermanence.

Understanding this puts a whole different angle on suffering or dukkah. We know dukkah's gonna happen. I love that scene in the movie Forrest Gump where he's jogging and he steps in a huge pile of crap. A fellow jogger is dismayed and feels really bad for Forrest, but he just looks over and shrugs and says "Shit Happens", and a famous bumper sticker is born. In fact, the entire movie is a lovely example of living in the moment, practicing non-attachment, and showing that life is suffering. Call it shit, call it suffering, call it dukkah, but whatever you call it – "IT" is going to happen.

Experiencing a loss is one of the more extreme forms of suffering that occurs in our lives, with some losses being more profound than others. It is during these times that we experience the reality that "life is suffering" most keenly, but it is also in these times that we recognize how powerful attachment can be and how it impacts our suffering.

This was never truer for me than when Don died. At the time of his death, I was very satisfied with my life. Don and I had been married for nearly 11 years, together for 13. I was building my massage therapy practice, and it was going well. We lived in a beautiful condo, a restored silk mill with soaring ceilings, huge sunlit windows, and views of the river. Don was preparing to retire from the company where he had worked for 30 years and we were looking forward to truly entering a new phase in our lives. Life was sweet. Nearly every day I would drive the few miles home from my office and think to myself how lucky I was, how fortunate.

And then it all changed in, literally, a heartbeat. Suffering was upon me in a way that I had never experienced before, nor could have even *imagined* experiencing. The scope and scale of it was beyond comprehension. Yet (as we all do), I carried on. It wasn't pretty, it wasn't brave, it wasn't poetic; it was survival pure and simple. With time, the intensity of the pain lessened but the core of the suffering remained. The only thing I wanted was the one thing I couldn't have – my life with Don, the way it was before he died.   Everything else that came after that did not compare to my old life – not the two new houses I bought, not the jobs I took (due to financial reasons I had to close my practice). The time I spent with family and friends served as more of a reminder of the way things *used to be* then a comfort and solace. I was taking suffering to new heights, making it an art form.   I cried, I raged, I drank, and I shopped.   Then I did the worst thing of all – I gave up. I began to believe what my suffering voice was telling me – "you're never going to be happy again", "you will always be alone", "you will have no money", and "there is no hope".

Hopelessness is a horrible place to be in. Never again will I question when someone tells me that their life feels hopeless. I understand that feeling now. But at some level I knew there had to be a way out. I had, after all, had glimmers of hope. There *were* days since Don had died that I laughed, days that I enjoyed outings with friends, days where I felt more positive than negative. But I struggled to hold onto those feelings, so the suffering returned.

It wasn't until my relocation to Maine and my participation in a book study group about Zen Buddhism where it finally dawned on me that the cause of my suffering was my attachment to my old life. Without a doubt it was a really shitty thing that Don had died when he did. Without a doubt it was really shitty that I had to close a business I loved, sell a home I loved, and take on work that paid the bills but was not enjoyable to me. Without a doubt it was shitty that I had to learn to live on a lot less money, and that my future financial state was less secure than it had been. It was all shitty. But it was nothing more than dukkah, and dukkah happens.   In spite of my best efforts to create a secure and stable life; it was all shattered in an instant, because that's just the way things are. Your life may be more charmed and secure than mine, or it may be much more horrible than mine, but dukkah happens.

And when dukkah happens, it's gonna hurt. Sometimes it hurts really badly, and it hurts for a long time. But we can lessen the pain by realizing that any comfort or security, happiness or joy that we may have been feeling before the dukkah happened was only temporary. Hopefully, we appreciated the good times while they were here, and hopefully we enjoyed the good times while they lasted because there was no way they were going to last forever; that is just the nature of things. Life is a wheel, and wheels are meant to turn. It's what wheels do. A wheel can no more deny its nature to turn than a fish can deny its nature to swim.

We exacerbate the suffering we experience when dukkah happens because we deny the nature of the universe; that everything is impermanent. All of our planning and striving cannot change this fundamental law. Because it is our nature to attach to our illusion of security, attach to the people with whom we are surrounded, attach to the idea that we can somehow, (if we work hard enough, plan enough, save enough)

protect ourselves and those we love from this universal law.

This realization was such an "aha" for me.   I finally

"got" that I was perpetuating my cycle of anger, frustration,

fear, and sadness (my suffering) with my attachment to my old

life.   Even more powerful was the realization that I could only

begin to be free of this suffering by accepting that the old life

was gone, and that I had to take responsibility for myself to

begin to create a new and different one.

Does that mean that I have made peace with my

dukkah? Not entirely, but I have gained a new and fresh

perspective on how to view suffering. Knowing that the bad

times are just as impermanent as the good times is very

powerful. Whenever, we crave or cling to something or

someone we are extending our suffering.   Desire, passion,

striving – these in and of themselves are not negatives.

However, when we become so attached to the object(s) or

person(s) of our desire and striving that we think we can't "live without them", then we have set ourselves up for suffering.

I don't know the nature of your loss; but having experienced my own, I know it was not easy and I know that, like me, you felt pain. I know you suffered and may still be suffering.   Now I encourage you to ask yourself "What am I attached to?"   When you honestly answer that question you can begin to explore what steps you need to take to release yourself from that attachment.

For me, the first step was acceptance that my old life was gone.   The second step was internalizing the reality that the nature of everything is impermanent.   With this understanding I could begin to move forward with a renewed sense of hope, and the knowledge that joy, happiness, and peace were emotions that I could once again experience.

"A" is for Anxiety

Anxiety: a painful or apprehensive uneasiness of mind over an impending or anticipated ill. Fearful, concern or interest.

I have never considered myself an anxious person. When fear and worry hit I approached it as another problem to be solved, another challenge to conquer. Sure, looming deadlines at work, personnel problems, and family issues sometimes kept me awake at night, but I always felt that I had the internal resources to face them, deal with them and move on.

Of course that all changed when Don died. Every single aspect of your life is changed with the death of a spouse: from your daily routine, to the meals you cook, to going from shared responsibilities and chores to doing everything yourself. From having a partner with whom you share the decision making process to making all the decisions yourself. From being a couple at parties and dinners with friends, to being a single. From sharing your bed to sleeping alone. Nothing is as it was. For me, even my work life changed thanks to a clumsy accident that left me unable to work for four months. My financial circumstances were further changed and challenged when the life insurance policy I was counting on using to pay off the mortgage was denied because it was still in the "contestability period".

Anxiety showed up with a vengeance. And I don't mean anxiety with a small "a", I'm talking about Anxiety with a capital "A".   The only thing that kept the anxiety at bay was the staggering grief and sadness over losing my partner and best friend.

The Anxiety was ferocious – it kept me up at night, it sat on my chest like a weight squeezing all the air out of me.   It made me dizzy, it sent my thoughts spiraling out of control; one thought racing with another, and then another, and another until my mind was just one confused mass of panic. It caused me to over think every decision, created self doubt, and crushed my self confidence. All of my emotions rode just beneath the surface.   I felt like I was wearing a thin and brittle veneer of a

mask that would crack at the slightest provocation.   I didn't

trust myself anymore; I didn't trust my reactions, and I certainly

didn't trust my intuition.   Before Don's death I had seen a

predictable and planned path to the future, after his death I saw

nothing.

What was going to become of me?   How was I going to

pay the bills? How would I manage on my own?   How was I

going to survive this?   The fire of panic fed itself in an endless

cycle. Occasionally the fire would die down, but the embers

glowed hot enough to be stirred back into a raging fire spurred

again by some random thought or event. It was unacceptable

to me that the life I had planned and crafted so carefully was

gone.   There were times that between the grief and the anxiety

I was certain that I too would die in my sleep; and to be

perfectly honest there were many times when that idea was

just fine by me.   It would have been much easier than having

to continue plodding forward feeling the way that I did.

As the weeks and months went by, I slowly came to resign myself to my new reality. I use the word "resign" and not "accept" deliberately here, because I believe they are two different things. Resignation to me is acceptance on a material level, but not on an emotional one. It would be several years before acceptance at the emotional level occurred.

With this resignation to the facts of my altered reality, I began to make decisions and choices. Doing so helped to ease the panic somewhat; as did keeping active, but the feelings of Anxiety about the future persisted. It didn't help matters that I was about to turn 50 the year that Don died. The fearlessness of my youth was behind me, and now it seemed that only a yawning chasm of uncertainty lay before me. There were two things that frightened me. The first was facing the future without Don. The second was financial. The financial safety net that I thought was going to be there in case of the unthinkable vanished, due to nothing more than bad timing.

Not helping my Anxiety about finances was the programming and attitude about money with which I had been raised. If there was ever anything that was drilled into me, it was about making sure you had enough money. It wasn't about having money so you could acquire material things, but it was about having money to cover emergencies, to pay the bills and to be SURE to have enough money to never BE DEPENDANT on anyone else. Of course in that environment, there was never such a thing as having "too much" money for these scenarios. In our house, fear of not having enough money even outweighed fear of going to hell, which was saying something.

I knew intellectually that this obsession about my financial future was doing nothing to address the problem, and it certainly wasn't helping me manage my Anxiety (with a capital "A"). I made the decisions I thought would help me. I sold the condo, paid off all my debts and bought a mobile home (cash). That was fine, except it turned out that I could not adapt to the train whistle blasting through the road crossing half a block away. Even after two years, the damn thing still startled the

crap out of me. I then sold the mobile and bought a small

house in a quiet neighborhood in my old home town.

However, buying that house took almost all my cash. The house

was old and the basement became a small river during heavy

rain.   Over the course of these years, my Anxiety levels went

up and down with my bank account; every unexpected bill was

a major stressor, and certain (in my mind) doom lay ahead.

One thing I did know was that this was NOT how I

wanted to live out the rest of my life.   I knew that the only

way that I was going to beat this thing was to make a drastic

change. Either I was going to need to find a way to generate

enough cash to erase the fear, or I was going to have to find a

better way to deal with the fear.

In the end it was the fear of living the way I was, with

Anxiety as my constant companion that outweighed the

financial fear.   Through my process of identifying "What Kind

of Life Do I Want", the most important thing became the desire to feel better.   So that was when I put my house on the market, sold it, put all the cash in the bank and moved to Maine. I set aside a chunk of the money from the sale of the house and told myself that when that was gone, I would go back to work.   I did work some of the time in Maine, which helped to offset the drain from my bank account.

That was how I faced my fear. I changed my dynamic with it. Instead of letting it rule my decisions, I decided to turn the tables on it by giving up some of so my called "security" (which wasn't making me feel secure anyway) in order to feel better.   And I resolved to leave that fear on the shelf while I dealt with other issues.   There were times that I felt incredibly selfish.   There were times I felt reckless about my choice.   But as time went by, I also found that I was feeling better.

I learned that Anxiety is best dealt with by being in the moment. I look back to that definition of anxiety: "impending or anticipated ill".   We never really think about that when we feel anxious, do we?   When we are consumed by Anxiety we are in the wrong moment; we are in a moment that has not yet come, and may in fact never come.

I still have moments of anxiety and panic. They tend to sneak up on me now; being there when I first wake up, or when I stop doing something in which I was completely absorbed. It's annoying as hell. But I'm better at recognizing it for what it is; worry about things that are not yet here. When that happens I use several strategies:

1. I remind myself that what I am fearful of has not yet occurred, and may never occur.
2. I take a deep breath and work to bring myself back into focus on the moment – take a walk, meditate, play with the cats, run the vacuum.
3. I remind myself that this feeling of panic is temporary, it *will* pass, and in fact it always does.

I still do long range planning. I'm not suggesting an "eat, drink and be merry" approach to life. What I am suggesting is perspective. Being present in each moment will help reduce your worry about the next moment, because you are getting through THIS moment just fine, aren't you? You are sitting here reading this book and no calamity is befalling you at THIS moment (unless you ignored that tornado warning) is it? And so the next moment will come and you will be in that moment as it happens, then that moment will pass and another one will take its place. Life is, after all, just a series of moments, one right after another.

I did not accomplish this alone. You should never, ever, feel guilty about seeking help when you are recovering from a loss. What worked for me may not work for you. Whatever help you do seek, make sure it is "healthy" help as opposed to unhealthy help like overeating, smoking, drinking yourself to sleep, or shopping away your fear. Choose your champions wisely and they will help you slay the dragon of fear and anxiety.

ALL WE CAN DO IS KEEP BREATHING

To be blunt, the first year after losing Don was horrible; and to be honest with you, the second year wasn't much better. Yet somehow my heart kept beating and my lungs kept taking in oxygen and expelling carbon dioxide. When I first wrote this it was a dark day. Even though the sun was shining I felt old and alone, and the times when I felt alone were the times when I felt afraid. I had learned, while watching the weather report that evening that another foot or more of snow was going to fall in the next 24 hours. This was on top of the 2 feet of snow we had accumulated less than 36 hours ago. We were going to have almost four feet of snow in four days. Here in the east we referred to these back to back storms as "Snowmaggedon". I had also just learned that I was going to owe $500 in Federal taxes; another hit to my dwindling bank account. My house was for sale, but needless to say between the economy and the snow, no one was looking at houses.

Times like these were where my panic seemed to snowball (no pun intended). I worried about getting to and from work because of the weather. I worried about having to move (by myself with only a snow shovel) two more feet of snow. If the office was closed because of the weather, I wouldn't get paid. And then, because the short term worrying wasn't stressful enough, I started playing the "What if" game. What if I can't support myself and I go broke? What if I need a new car? What if I can't pay my taxes? What if, what if? All the while my breathing became more shallow, and more hurried.

I hated those "What if" days. But once I had run the gamut of all the "what ifs" I could think of, it dawned on me that they were all negatives. What is it about human nature that we seem to shift into negative thought patterns when we feel stressed? Why do we assume that only bad things are going to happen to us and assume defeat? Certainly, some of this thinking was a result of the "recentcy effect". After all, less than two years ago I had experienced the worst thing that had ever happened to me – I found my husband dead.

I took a deep breath. I watched the birds and squirrels happily gobbling food from the feeders I had tromped through the snow earlier that day to fill. I took another deep breath, it felt good. Some days when we are grieving a loss that is all we can do; take a deep breath. One after another. I thought about how to turn my "what if" thinking into something more positive. What if I won the lottery? What if I found a second shift job that allowed me to sleep in late? What if I used the extra time I had to exercise more (other than to shovel snow)? I kept breathing. I thought about taking a pragmatic approach to my "what if" state of mind. This snow will melt and spring will come. If I don't sell this place, I'll stay here. I may have to look for another job with more hours - so what? My thoughts drifted and I was reminded of the opening for the long running soap opera "Days of Our Lives", with the hour glass and the ticking clock music and the dramatic voice overdub saying something about "the sands of times....." I took another deep breath and looked out the window, it had started snowing again.

Life is only going one direction, forward. There are fewer grains of sand in my hourglass of life today then there were yesterday. How do I choose to spend it? Worrying about tomorrow? A day that will either take care of itself when it gets here or not at all.

At the time of his death, Don had been sober for 21 years, during those which he was an active member in Alcoholics Anonymous. Perhaps their most famous saying is "One Day At A Time". Dealing with loss is a lot like that. It is enough to handle what is coming at you today – the emotions, the decisions you need to make, the change in your routines – that is all quite enough for *this* day. Living one day at a time doesn't mean you are reckless about life, or that you shirk your responsibilities, or that you spend all of your savings. It doesn't mean that you *never* think about tomorrow in terms of your health, your desires, and your finances. I do think it means that we focus on making today the best possible day; even if that means facing another snowstorm, or tax payment, an uncertain housing future, and a less than satisfactory job situation. And we keep breathing.

KEEPING IT SIMPLE

We humans have a penchant for making life more complicated than it needs to be. Perhaps our ancestors fell into the same patterns, but for many centuries most of humanity was too preoccupied with surviving. I doubt they had either the time or energy to engage in emotional behaviors that complicated their lives.

On the other hand, our society here in the west seems to thrive on complication. Our relationships are complicated, our schedules are complicated, our laws are complicated, our politics are complicated, and don't even get me started on the tax code here in the USA.

As a result, we have very little time to sit back and take a deep breath. Little time to allow ourselves to think about why or how our lives got so complicated and what, if anything, we want to do to change that. Some people seem to thrive on chaos. They like to be busy, and they like to always have several projects in the hopper, calendars packed with kids' activities, outings with friends, meetings and committees.   If this works for them and they feel that their lives are fulfilled and authentic, then I say "more power to 'em, go in peace my friend.".   The opposite of this are those of us who deliberately don't schedule anything, don't get involved, but instead fill our time with television, books, internet, movies and video games.

"I like to keep busy" is a response that most people give me when I comment on how full their lives are. But why do so many of us feel compelled to "keep busy"?   When does busyness become a code word for distraction? When does TV watching become a euphemism for escaping discomfort and dissatisfaction with ourselves? When does filling our lives up with activity and acquisition of "things" become grasping and yearning for something that we can't define?   And on the other side, when does seclusion become escape?

One of my goals for my "Year in Maine" was to look for ways to simplify my life. This included eliminating television and newspapers, reducing my living space from a house to a small studio apartment, living in a town where I could walk for most goods and services, and using nature as my primary form of "entertainment". Part of this was by design; after all, I had come here to "reconnect with life", and so it was important for me to eliminate distractions. The second reason was financial. Not knowing if I wanted to work during my time here and not knowing whether or not I could *find* work during my time here meant that my endeavor needed to be a frugal one.

My experiment with keeping it simple was both rewarding and challenging. Challenging, because our culture is so conditioned to think that feeling uncomfortable is "bad", that we seek out distractions when confronted with thoughts and feelings that are unpleasant. Sometimes "the truth" isn't easy to hear even when we proclaim that we want to hear it.   I certainly found this to be true. There were days when I had to allow those negative thoughts and feelings to come and go, and find positive ways to deal with them when they did come (like hiking). My experiment with keeping it simple was also rewarding, because learning to live with less – less stuff, less technology, fewer conveniences - provided me with opportunities to be more present in each moment, to slow down long enough to listen to that still, small voice inside of me that, when I allow it to speak, will help to point me in the right direction.

It took several months, and many days of hiking in Acadia for me to hear what my still, small voice was telling me over and over.   Like the realization that some questions have no answers. Deep down, I already knew this. But when confronted with the loss of my husband, I craved answers more than ever.   Just as not all questions have answers, I also came to realize that not every problem has a solution. My mantras of "Make it happen", "Just do it", and "I will find a way to get what I want", along with a core belief that if I am "good", then good things will happen to me proved to be seriously flawed when confronted with loss.   The crowning realization was that I was not always going to get what I wanted, because what I wanted back was my old life with my husband, and unless I could find a way to transport myself to a parallel universe, that wasn't going to happen. Not only was I not going to get back the love of my life, but my socio-economic status was altered as well. I was going to have to accept (among other things) having less money in the bank, being a sole supporter, eating out less, traveling less, and driving an older car. While my friends and family went merrily on about their lives (or so it seemed), everything about my life had been altered.

It really IS that simple. We don't always get what we want. Life isn't fair, and you had better consider yourself fortunate to have had the life you had for as long as you had it (when compared to most of the people in this world). I don't say this to minimize your loss or my own, because that loss was the single most difficult and painful thing I am likely to have to face in this lifetime. But I am here to tell you that whatever it is, it is survivable.

Along the way I learned that simplifying my life had other benefits. I found out that things I thought I wanted and needed (like cable TV) really weren't all that important to me. I found out that spending three hours hiking is really a lot more rewarding then spending three hours in the front of the television. I found out that reading a classic novel is more rewarding than watching the Hollywood version of it and eating a big bucket of greasy popcorn along the way. I found out that listening to a dedicated group of high school students play classical music at a free concert is just as enjoyable as listening to a paid symphony orchestra. I learned that having a few outfits I really like is more satisfying (and much less stressful) then standing in front of a closet full of clothes and trying to figure out what to wear. And I found out that being alone doesn't have to mean that I am lonely. Put simply (no pun intended), simplifying my life reduced my stress and improved my mental, physical, and emotional health.

Stripping away unnecessary and distracting activities helped me face these realities in a way that I don't think I could have achieved had I not removed myself from the distractions of work, family and friends, social activities, television, eating out, maintaining a house, shopping, and a host of other things.

I encourage you to simplify your life where and whenever you can. In doing so you'll strip away all the "crap" that is distracting you from what is real. Because while the truth is hard (life isn't fair and you won't always get what you want), so is the truth beautiful. Because the truth is, it's all temporary. And when we embrace this truth we can identify what is most precious to us and appreciate it while we can.

THE CONTROL ILLUSION

Nothing shatters the illusion that you have control over your life more than a major loss. I actually puzzled over whether to use the word *illusion* or *delusion* for the title of this essay. In the final analysis, I'd have to say that when it comes to control, it is a bit of both, but for the purposes of this discussion I settled on illusion.

Control is a seductive state of being, and it is especially powerful in Western cultures. We are brought up with the notion (which is reinforced by advertising and the images all around us), that if we just work hard enough, stay out of trouble, and try to do the right thing; we will have a good life, be successful, and happy. Good things happen to good people, right? We walk around with the attitude that certainly bad things happen in the world, but they happen to other people, not to me. If I manage my money, love my family, go to church (at least on Christmas and Easter), act grateful, go to my job every day (even when I'm sick), throw my spare change in the red buckets at the holidays, send a check to earthquake victims, or post a poignant meme on Facebook; well, then certainly I'm controlling my life and only good will come of it, right? Wrong.

As I write this, it is a few weeks after the latest mass shooting to occur in the United States. It was a particularly horrific one this time, with twenty seven victims, twenty of them young children. The scale and scope of this tragedy shattered (or should have shattered) any illusion that any of us had about being in control of our lives. Here was a community filled with decent, hardworking people, solidly middle class; the American dream personified. There is no doubt in my mind that if you had interviewed and asked the members of this community the day before the shooting occurred if they were in control of their lives, they would have answered in the affirmative; with perhaps just a few caveats thrown in. But in a matter of moments, a deeply disturbed young man with tremendous fire power at his fingertips destroyed any illusion these people had of being in control of their lives.

Of course in the days and weeks that followed, the community, the nation, and in fact, the world attempted to explain why "we" had lost control of this situation. Everything from ready access to certain types of guns and ammunition, a flawed and failed mental health care system, lack of prayer in schools, violence in movies and video games; how hard we worked to find a scapegoat. There were pictures posted on-line of children running into the arms of Jesus in heaven; another attempt at control – for if "we" are not in control, then surely there must be some divine being out there that **is** in control, for how else could such a terrible thing happen?

Terrible things DO happen. They happen to good people, they happen to bad people. They happen to rich people, they happen to poor people. But this isn't about "dukkah" (that's another essay); this is about recognizing that any control you think you have over life is an illusion. It is an extremely powerful illusion, but an illusion none the less.

I feel fairly well qualified to speak to this, because I am, as I like to refer to myself, a recovering control freak. I was extremely skilled at bringing order to chaos. In fact that was one way that I marketed myself to potential employers. I enjoyed nothing more than stepping into a mess and figuring out how to restore order, how to organize, how to put in place systems and procedures, policies, and practices that would prevent the chaos from occurring again.   My home life was equally organized, with work, family and fun neatly compartmentalized into their respective "buckets".   My jobs during those years required me to think on my feet and shift gears quickly to situations and problems as they arose. So keeping order and control where I could made the stress easier to deal with.

When I decided to leave my career in Human Resources Management that also was a well controlled transition.   Bills were paid off, expenses were lowered, and goals for starting my own business were established.   I was feeling connected to the universe in a way I had not experienced before, I was practicing positive affirmations, I was focused, determined; and oh yes, I was in control of my own destiny.

But just like the folks of the Newtown, CT tragedy, the morning I walked into the bedroom and found my husband dead, any illusion that I had control over my life vanished, although it would take several months for this fact to register in my consciousness. As I watched my financial security net evaporate, as I watched my livelihood suspended due to injury, and as I continued to try and grasp the reality that the love of my life and my best friend,(a seemingly healthy man) had suddenly died; the dawning realization that control was an illusion became clear. The tighter I tried to hold on, the more I tried to regain some semblance of order in my life, the more apparent the illusion became.

I did not go quietly into this new reality.   I battled it with everything I had. I raged, I cried, I screamed, I argued.   As much as I grieved the loss of the man I loved, I grieved equally the loss of my illusions.   All my well laid plans, all my (or so I thought) preparedness for the unthinkable, all my organization were no match for the reality that for years I had simply been deluding myself about being in control. It was all just smoke and mirrors.

Some people find comfort in shifting the responsibility for control to something or someone outside of themselves. "It's all in God's hands", or "The Universe knows what it is doing" are two of my favorite mantras of the newly traumatized.   I've generally maintained an attitude that a person can believe what they want to believe, and as long as it isn't hurting them or anyone else, as long as they aren't trying to push their belief system off on me then if it helps you, go for it.

But, honestly, I have to say that I find this abdication of control to be a big part of how we delude ourselves about the realities of how the universe works.   It's just another way of keeping the light on at night so the monsters can't get us. If *we* can't control things, well let's just hope and pray that there's someone "out there" who can.

Difficult as it was (and is); I prefer to acknowledge the fact that any control that I think I may be exerting in my life is just an illusion. It is a gift, a fortunate circumstance that today life is going the way I want and that events are unfolding the way I expect them to.   As much as I might want to think that it is my extraordinary planning and organizational skills; my discipline and determination, my charm and agreeable personality that are causing things to happen in a certain way, it is really just luck. There are days when I find myself sliding back into the clutches of the illusion, because it is powerful, seductive, and comforting. All we need to do is look at the people around us to see this demonstrated everyday in our own lives and the lives of others. Some achieve satisfaction from perpetuating the illusion for themselves alone; others try to extend the illusion by exerting influence and control on the people around them.   It is like a drug, the more control we (think we) have, the better we (think we) feel.

Have you ever seen a magic show?   I think these days magicians refer to themselves as illusionists, which is a more definitive title. They devise clever and complex mechanical devices to fool us into thinking that they've sawed their assistant in half or made an elephant disappear. They distract us so that we look away at the crucial moment and we miss the sleight of hand that occurs.   The illusionist is a good metaphor for how we approach life. We become the master illusionist in our own lives and are devastated when the show ends and we learn that there wasn't really any magic, and that we weren't in control after all.

So what do we do with this new reality? How do we successfully function? Of course we need (most of us) to keep schedules, to organize our time.   Of course it is useful to set

goals, to write "to do" lists. Of course it is prudent to manage

and save money, to hope for and assume that we are going to

live long, happy, and productive lives.   The key is to not fall into

the trap, to not get sucked back into the illusion.   Recognize

and accept that anything that is going well in your life is less

about what and how you are doing things and more about good

fortune. I hear your brain turning as you read this. You don't

want to accept it, it can't be true.   You are fighting to keep that

beautiful illusion going.

In the next minute any number of things could occur to

shatter your illusion.   Your house could explode due to a gas

line break, killing you instantly.   The phone could ring telling

you your spouse has been in an accident.   Your parent could

suddenly be struck with a stroke.   Your employer could tell

you that you've been laid off.   A crazed person could walk into

your child's school and start shooting.   It isn't just the big

things, the major catastrophes which will shake us from our

illusion. It's the little things too. The car breaks down, we drop the cell phone in the toilet, our child pukes all over us as we go to walk out the door, or we run out of coffee.

No one wants to live in fear, and I'm not suggesting that you do.   Living a life controlled by fear is just as unhealthy as walking around thinking you are in control.   I am a Star Trek fan going back to the original television show.   In one of the movies (that had *both* Captain James T. Kirk and Jean Luc Picard), the plot contained a place called the Nexus which the villain was trying to get to, by any means possible.   The reason that the Nexus was so desirable was that because once you were in the Nexus you could spend eternity living the life you had always imagined you would live.   It was a place where all mistakes and regrets vanished; a place of the ultimate "do over".   The Nexus was an eternal control illusion.

Letting go of our control illusion is a scary process.   It feels as though we are walking a tightrope without a net, but the reality is that there is no net. Are you ready to give up your illusion or do you want fate to do it for you? Or, will you

choose to shatter the illusion of control yourself, and, in doing

so, begin to more fully live each precious moment as it is given

to you? In this you do have control. The choice is yours.

WHAT IS TRUE?

"If you cannot find the truth right where you are, where else do you expect to find it?"   Dogen

In my Dharma (Zen Buddhism) class, there was an opportunity during each class for members to share insights that they had gained since the previous class, or to share how what we had learned, thus far, was helping us on a daily basis.

One of the principles that people felt easy and helpful to apply in their lives was the "What is True" question.   This question is used when we are faced with stressful and unpredictable people and events.   It is a simple way to diffuse emotionally charged situations when you may feel tempted to lash out or respond in an emotional way to what is happening. It is by no means the only tool available in these circumstances, but it seemed to be one that people remembered and found easy to implement.

As I have mentioned before, one of my greatest anxieties after Don died had to do with money and how to earn it. Would I have enough, would I be able to find work, would I

have the stamina to work full time again after working part time

for so many years? What if I had to spend all of my savings?

The litany of questions and worry ran on and on. I constructed

endless variations of budget spreadsheets on my computer.

This worry about money was an inbred characteristic, finely

honed over several generations.   The fact that I was now on

my own, with no partner to serve as financial back-up, only

made matters worse.

This chronic worry provided the ideal situation for me

to practice the "What is True" question. When I would feel the

crush of anxiety bearing down on me, I would stop, take a

breath and ask myself: What is True? What is true about this

situation? What is true about my worry *today?*   Bringing the

worry into the present reminded me that *today* I was not broke,

today I was still able to work, *today* I did have a plan for how to

maximize the money I had, and *right now* there was no crisis happening that required me to use money that I had not planned for.

A couple of years after Don's death I ran across a wonderful book called "Rowing the Atlantic". It was written by Roz Savage, a woman about 10 years younger than me, who had quit her IT management job, ended an unhappy marriage, and gave up financial security to "find herself". What she ended up doing was participating in a race rowing across the Atlantic Ocean......alone. It took her nearly 100 days, and she certainly didn't win the race, but she found her purpose on that ocean. She went on to become the first woman to row solo across three oceans; the Atlantic, the Pacific, and the Indian, and became an environmental crusader for the health of our oceans (and the environment in general). Her story is both engaging and inspirational.

One of the things I learned from reading Roz's story is that when you are on the ocean, in a boat powered only by you rowing it, you get very skilled at dealing with "What is true".

Moment by moment she had to focus on whatever task was at hand; whether it was fixing a broken oar, keeping the cabin of her small boat dry, or dealing with days when the current took her backwards, forcing her to re-row the same miles she had rowed the day before. Thinking ahead on the ocean would only get her into trouble because in spite of the technology she had at her disposal; satellite radio, weather data and so on, the ocean was unpredictable. So she dealt with *what was true* in the present, moment by moment.

One of the other important things (and there were many) that I learned from Roz's experience was that when you are faced with something that seems insurmountable, to think in terms of taking small steps. Ask yourself "What is the first thing that I need to do to accomplish my goal, overcome my challenge, and achieve my dream"? Going back to my example of financial worries, one of the first steps I could take was to make sure that my resume was up to date. Other examples would be to look for opportunities to reduce my expenses; such as shopping at thrift stores or canceling magazine subscriptions (you can borrow them for free at your local library). This idea of finding that first small step to solving a problem or achieving a goal is another way of keeping yourself in the present and focusing on the *now* rather than worrying about the future.

The *"what is true"* question is a technique that is designed to help you deal with anxiety and emotionally charged situations where worrying about the future, obsessing about a problem, or where negative emotions are threatening to carry you away. Asking the question "what *is true*" will help bring your attention back to the here and now. By asking and answering this question moment by moment, we can get through the moment at hand and each future moment as it becomes the present.

IS THIS AS GOOD AS IT GETS?

"To understand everything is to forgive everything."

(Buddha)

I sometimes think it would be interesting to have a "class reunion" of sorts with the people that were attending the grief support group I attended in the first 12 – 18 months after Don died. It would be interesting to see how they have managed to reconstruct their lives in the intervening years. The group in which I participated was specifically for people who, like me, had lost a spouse. I wonder how many remarried, how many moved out of the area, how many changed careers, sold their homes. I wonder how many of them are satisfied with their current lives versus just making the best of it. I wonder how many, like me, still have times when they struggle. Would such a reunion make me feel better or worse about myself? Would I feel like I was the only one in the group who hadn't successfully moved on?

There are times when I do ask myself: "Is this as good as it gets"? Times when I am frustrated with my lack of enthusiasm for life, my slipping back into bad habits, my battle with gaining weight and losing it, my battle with drinking too much too often, my battle with anxiety. It didn't help that Don passed away just about the same time that menopause hit. Certainly I knew that the heat flashes were related to my depleted estrogen levels, but the mental fog, fatigue, mood swings and anxiety; were they a factor of menopause or a factor of grieving, or both?

I actually hesitated to include this essay because I didn't want a person reading this who had recently suffered a loss to think "oh my god, does this process (of grieving) drag on *forever*?!" But, I also wanted to be honest about my experiences. There are days still when I feel hopeless, when I am anxious about the future, when I 'm totally frustrated with myself, and days when I fall into despair realizing that more of life is behind me than ahead of me.

Don represented an anchor for me. People hear the word "anchor" and they tend to have a negative connotation with the word. Anchor to me represents a stabilizing factor, something that keeps you from drifting in the wrong direction. It was a role that Don and I were able to play in one another's lives. When he died I felt that I was set adrift, caught up in currents which I was unable to navigate alone. I felt I was a better person as a result of having Don in my life and when he was gone I found it difficult to hang onto those finer aspects of myself. For me, a big part of recovering was to discover a way to become my own "anchor". The bottom line is that whatever, or whomever, you have lost, part of who you are today is a by-product of that person or situation having been in your life.

If you do an on line search of "What does it mean to recover from grief", you will find a wealth of articles on the topic and a variety of definitions. The definition that makes the most sense to me is the one that says that we would not *choose* to have the loss, but that we no longer fight it. We begin to reinvest emotional energy into new goals, people, projects and interests.

I like that definition because it doesn't mean that you are never going to have moments of sadness. It doesn't mean that you will never miss the person, relationship, job, or home that you lost. It doesn't mean that in the case of a death that you forget about the person you lost or act like they never existed.

Successful recovery also extends beyond asking and answering the question: "What can I learn from this?" That is especially true in the case of the death of a loved one. Who wants to learn how to deal with the loss of someone whom we loved so very much and wanted to be in our lives "forever"? No one wants this! And yet, loss is a part of the human experience, regardless of how much we try to insulate ourselves from it.

When the bad days come, when we find ourselves asking "Is this as good as it gets", it is especially important that we try to stay in the present moment.   Because asking "is this as good as it gets?" is really just anxiety about the future.   You may be sad, you may be missing what you lost, and you may be frustrated, angry, or dejected;   but it is only a moment in time, and it will pass.   Acknowledge what you are feeling by saying: "This is sadness" or "this is frustration", and then let it go.

Recovery does not mean that you forget. It does not mean that you will always be "happy" or that you will never feel pain. There will be things that remind you; a song, a smell, a location, old friends.   There will be events when you will feel sadness that the person missing is not able to share that moment with you.   For me, one of the most difficult things is realizing again and again that Don's grandchildren will never have an opportunity to meet him and to experience the wonderful person he was. As thrilled as I was to spend a year living in Maine, there were many times when I thought about how much Don would have loved being there with me, and how he would have thrown himself into the experience of living there.

Be prepared to experience those "are this as good as it gets?" moments.   Practice self compassion. I do this by reminding myself that those moments are normal, and that they serve to reinforce and remind me of how important Don was to me. When you have lost someone you loved a great deal, the mourning never goes away entirely. I also ask myself if my actions and reactions to him not being here honor his memory and his life.   During the dark moments it can be difficult to think of this, because, after all, that person is gone and if they can "see" what you are doing, would they really care?   Regardless of what you believe or don't believe about the afterlife, I think there is value in considering our actions in relationship to someone who mattered so much to us. The fact that they are no longer here should not diminish our desire to have them be proud of us. When we are struggling, external motivation such as this can be more effective than internal

motivation.   For whatever reason, we will do for others what

we are unable to do for ourselves.

I don't know *if or when* we stop asking: "Is this as good

as it gets"?   My experience is that as time goes by, the

question becomes less frequent, the dark periods shorter, and

the pain less intense.   Loss is a part of being human, and since

humans are by definition imperfect creatures, our grieving

process will not be a perfect one.   It will be as unique as you

are.   And while your grief journey will be yours alone, take

comfort in knowing that you are not alone, for every other

human being will at some point be taking the same journey.

WHO AM I?

"I yam what I yam"

Popeye, the sailor man

This may be the mother lode of all questions asked since the beginning of time, along with the companion question "Why Am I Here?"

During a meditation workshop I attended, the leader of workshop challenged us to "sit" with the question "Who am I" during the session. The exercise was designed to help us learn how to keep the mind from straying by bringing our attention back to this question when we found our minds beginning to wander. The goal was less about getting an answer and more about learning how to focus.

However, when our minds are given a question it is human nature to try and answer said question. My answers that day were simple and surprising. Phrases such as "Who Cares?", and "Don't Know" were common refrains throughout the morning. I didn't spend time processing those answers

110

immediately; just wrote them down on an index card and filed them away for future contemplation.

Who Am I? Probably 99% of people when asked that question will answer by rattling off a litany such as: "I am a wife, a mother, a grandmother, a bank teller, a girl scout leader, a democrat", or "I am a husband, a software developer, a golfer, a softball coach" and so on.   This is not who we are at all, it is WHAT we are. This thinking is extended to others.   If I asked you "Who is Brad Pitt", you will likely respond: "He is an actor, he is with Angelina Jolie, he is a father, he is a good looking man" and so on. If I ask you "Who is the Dali Lama?" you will likely respond: "He is a Buddhist, a spiritual leader, an old man with funny glasses, a wise man, a Nobel prize peace recipient", etc. Again, these answers say nothing about "who" these two people are, but *what* we perceive them to be.   The answers that we give for ourselves and others when confronted with the "Who Am I" question are nothing more than labels.

These labels can exude great power over us. We let them define us; we let them dictate how we should act, what we should say, who our friends should be, and what things we should buy because we think that the labels represent who we are. It is also a way of letting the people we meet and interact with evaluate us to see if we conform to their idea of what is normal, what is acceptable, and decide whether or not we are someone they want to associate with.

This habit of using labels to define who we are can be extremely damaging. We use them to damage ourselves: "I am stupid, I am a failure, I am ugly". We also allow others to use them to do damage to us: "You are no good, you are fat, you are lazy, and you embarrass me". Labels are powerful and, repeated often enough, they become our reality and we think "this really *is* who I am". We also use labels to define others both positively and negatively "He's a thief, she's a drunk, he's a millionaire, she's beautiful, he's a loser, she's successful". So we careen through life, accumulating labels and thereby creating our answer to the question "Who Am I".

Here is a sample of the labels I collected over the years assigned by myself and others:

- Child
- Imaginative
- Petite
- Short
- Girlfriend
- Secretary
- Christian
- Daydreamer
- Rebellious
- Stubborn
- Independent
- Manager
- Friend
- Wife

- Executive

- Smart

- Overweight

- Embarrassing

- Divorcee

- Step-Mother

- Aunt

- Ambitious

- Classic Bitch

- Massage Therapist

- Flakey

- Widow

Of all the labels I accumulated over the years, the one I got most attached to was "widow". Perhaps because it represented the most traumatic event in my life, it was the label that I allowed to define me in the years after Don's death. At times it almost became part of my introduction as in, "Hi, my name is Carol and I'm a widow". Was it a ploy for sympathy?

Was it a way of lowering others expectations of me? Was it a way to explain my behavior, moods, and decisions?   Or, was it simply my way of attempting to redefine "who" I was?   I used to be this (wife), and now I am this (widow).   For me those two labels unconsciously represented all the things that had changed about me. "Wife" became the equivalent to "I am confident, I am loved, I am secure, I am safe, I am satisfied", and "Widow" became the equivalent to "I am scared, I am confused, I am lonely, I am sad". Being a widow became my explanation (or excuse) for not doing certain things or not making changes. "I can't handle stress, I can't sleep, I can't date, I can't lose weight, I can't be happy, I don't have money, I'm too tired, and I'm broken and nothing can fix me."

At first I wore this label like one of the ribbons that people wear to show they support a certain cause. As time went by, the label became more subtle but still remained a part of my daily dialogue with myself, and it continued to be a big part of how I defined myself to others.   I am not suggesting that I, or

115

anyone else, should hide being a widow or widower, but if like me, the label defines you to the point where it influences your decisions and actions, then I would suggest it has become a negative influence in your life.

In order for my healing to really begin, I needed to let go of the "widow" label along with ALL of the labels I was using. Because the reality was that none of them were "who I was".

Who Am I? I am a person. I am a human being with all the complexities that go along with it. That is the sum total of who I am. Why must we define ourselves further?   What does it matter? Who cares? All I should care about is looking at each person I encounter as being a person, a human being with all the complexities that go along with it.   When I release myself and others from labels that do nothing more than define *what* they are, then I am free to interact with them on a human to human level, listen to their stories, and enjoy their uniqueness and authenticity.

Being authentic is a hot topic. Books and articles abound on the subject of "being authentic" and "how to *become* more authentic". Let me simplify it for you. You and I are already authentic. I am authentic simply by existing. When I apply a label to myself and others, I impose limits and restrictions on the potential of our humanness. Letting go of labels allows us to live a more authentic life.

Who am I? I don't know. I don't know because I am changing. Because I am a human being with all the complexities that go along with it, and I am changing from moment to moment. Who I was yesterday, is not who I am today and not who I will be tomorrow. With each passing moment I experience new things, I meet new people, I think new thoughts, and I eat new foods. My mind and body is a constantly changing organism. Revel in this ambiguity. Allow yourself to jump into the flow of change.

Who is Brad Pitt? A person, a human being with all the complexities that go along with it. Who is the Dali Lama? A person, a human being with all the complexities that go along with it. Who is your spouse? Who is your co-worker? Who is your child? Who is your parent? Who is your neighbor? Who is your friend? Who is the homeless man on the corner? Who is the person that just cut you off on the freeway? Who are you?

The answer is always the same. Who we are is not a collection of labels. We can use labels to explain *what we* are, what roles we play in life, how we spend our time, what we enjoy doing. We can use them to explain our goals, dreams, hopes and fears. But don't let them define you, don't let them limit you. A label is only a word; it has only as much power as you give it. As I learned, labels can change in a heartbeat. Wife- heartbeat- widow.

Let me take this moment to acknowledge and honor who you are, who you were, and who you are becoming. Let me encourage you to let go of your attachment to the labels that you are allowing to define you. Release them and embrace your

authenticity.

Namaste

KEEP WALKING

"I will not move from this place until I solve my problem"

Buddha

I imagine that the above quote is rather "westernized"
for the purposes of clarity. But the message behind this quote
is that when the Buddha began his quest to understand why
suffering was part of life he did not rest until he attained
enlightenment. Before he began to meditate under the
infamous bodhi tree, he undertook the arduous life of an
aesthetic. This included extreme depravation in many forms
including sleep and food. The idea was that by depriving the
body, the mind would be clear and could become enlightened.
After several years he realized that this path was not leading
him to his truth. He also knew that the opulent and sheltered
life he had known in the palace was not enlightenment either.
So by the time he chose to sit under the tree and meditate he
was no doubt frustrated and feeling hopeless. However, he was
also persistent, and determined that if he sat in meditation long

enough he would find the answers he was seeking.   He did, and today we are able to study and benefit from his wisdom and teachings.

I can relate to his feelings of frustration. After four years of grieving my loss, I was still feeling anxious, depressed and angry.   I was determined to use my move to Maine as a vehicle to propel me out of that malaise and chart a new and more positive direction. Acadia National Park was going to be my backyard. With a ten minute drive I could be hiking along the ocean, around a lake, over a mountain, or through quiet woods.   Some trails were even within walking distance of my apartment.

I arrived in Maine at the end of November, a month after all the tourists have left the area. After an early October snowfall, this area of Maine experienced a much milder than usual winter, so with the exception of a few weeks in January, there were numerous trails and roads that I could safely hike all winter long.   Prior to coming to Maine, I wasn't really much of a hiker. I had gotten into decent shape earlier that year as part of an effort to lose weight, and I was eager to explore the miles of trails and carriage roads the park offered. I was also eager to have the opportunity to photograph the beauty of Acadia through all of its seasons, so this gave me extra incentive to get out there even on the coldest of days. So with new hiking boots, long underwear and a warm winter jacket I was ready to hit the trails.

I set a goal for myself to hike fifteen miles a week. Most weeks, I was able to reach this goal. I was able to log additional miles thanks to the walk-friendly nature of Bar Harbor, the town in which I lived. A grocery store, drug store, library, yoga studio, bank, doctors and hair salons were all less than a mile from where I lived; so walking became my primary mode of transportation. The joke became that I put gas in my car once a month "whether it needed it or not".

Aside from the convenience of walking for goods and services, and the pleasure of being able to photograph Acadia in all seasons, my walking served primarily as a meditative and healing exercise. Henry David Thoreau was on to something when he moved to, and subsequently wrote his famous "On Walden's Pond". Removing one's self from the mainstream, observing nature and listening to its inherent wisdom can prove to be a great teacher and healer.

I found this to be true for myself. As the weeks and months went by I developed clarity of thought and focus. When I felt the anxiety and depression returning, I would strap on the hiking boots and go. My mantra became: *I will keep walking until I feel better.* I became determined in this endeavor. The more I walked the better I felt. When I first got to Maine, a two mile walk was a long walk for me. When I left a year later it was six miles. I learned that with patience and persistence I could hike longer distances and over more challenging terrain than I ever thought possible. I hiked up hills and over mountains that I had only driven by in previous years of vacationing at Acadia. I had always felt embraced by the spirit of the place, but I now felt that Acadia was a part of me, that it had something to teach me, if I would only let myself be taught.

So I kept walking. I walked along the water, around lakes and ponds. I walked through woods and over mountains, through meadows and marshes. I walked in fresh snow along the Atlantic Ocean, and in the rain and fog over Jordan Pond. I walked at sunrise and sunset, on calm sunny days, and on days when I thought the wind would blow me off the mountainside. I walked on pavement, on crushed gravel roads, soft needled trails and rocky paths.

I kept walking. I watched and I listened. I watched otters swim and eagles soar. I watched bare trees bud and leaf out, display their fall colors and become bare once again. I watched seagulls dive for food and deer graze. I listened to wind blow and surf crash. I listened to rain fall and ice melt. I breathed in air that was tinged with salt and pine. I was patient, I was persistent and I was determined. I was going to keep walking until I felt better.

Along the way I gradually let go of the illusion that I could control life. I let go of the expectation that life *owed* me something. I accepted that life is suffering and I accepted my role in creating and extending my own suffering through my attachment to my old life, ideas, and expectations - of myself and of others. I learned that I was uniquely different from everyone else, but that I was also the same. I accepted that everything changes and nothing is permanent. I learned that when I paid attention to being in each moment that life was easier; free of worry and anxiety. I walked nearly 800 miles during that year.

The walks at my current home are different. There is less public land so I have to drive longer distances to find decent trails. The terrain is flat and there is less variety. But I keep walking, I will persist, I will continue to listen and I will continue to learn.

WHAT DO YOU HOPE TO ACCOMPLISH
WITH ALL THAT THINKING?

While hiking along the ocean one morning, I was thinking about the difficulty I was having with sitting and meditating on a regular basis. Meditating is one of those things that I have felt for many years would help reduce my stress, help me sleep better, and generally enhance my life. I would do it on occasion, or I would get off to a great start, but as soon as it became difficult (like after 15 minutes) I would abandon meditation as not really being "my thing". I had dozens of excuses; no time, no cushion, my feet went to sleep, the cats interrupted me, I would fall asleep, and so on.

Although the excuses persisted, so did the idea that regular meditation would be helpful in my quest for making peace with my loss. After getting to know a group of people who meditated routinely and listening to them talk about what their practice meant to them, I became more convinced that this was something I should make a commitment to doing.

In early spring of 2012, after a few weeks of what can only be described as sporadic meditation sessions of 10 – 20 minutes, I signed up for a half day workshop of yoga and meditation. Not only was I confident that this workshop would really help me "jumpstart" my meditation practice, I just *knew* it was going to be a relaxing and satisfying experience. After all, it was an hour of yoga, an hour of discussion and teaching, and less than two hours of seated and walking meditation – piece of cake, right?

If ever the phrase "simple, but not easy" when used to describe the practice of mediation was appropriate, it was certainly true for what I experienced that morning. Rather than being a relaxing and calming experience, I found myself overwhelmed by a flood of emotion. In addition, during the longer periods of seated meditation my legs became totally numb to the point where I was unable to even stand on them. During the break (by which point I had recovered the use of my legs), it took all of my will power not to walk out of the studio and never return.   After all, I lamented to the instructor, I had come to Maine to *feel better, not worse*.

I did decide to stay that morning and complete the workshop even though it took me several days to recover from the experience both physically and emotionally.   It would be six more months before I worked up the courage to resume a regular mediation practice.   It also took a few months to figure out that the tsunami of emotion I experienced that day was another important step in my healing process.

For most of my adult life, I had worked very hard at thinking my way out of problems. I was a master of compartmentalization. The emotional component(s) of the problem were placed into one compartment, the problem itself into another compartment.   I thought I was detaching from the problem emotionally, but what I was often doing was denying or suppressing the emotions associated with the problem. Needless to say, this approach was not very effective when confronted with the emotions tied to the loss of my husband.

Here was a problem that was ALL about emotion, and my tried and true method was no match for the range and power of the emotions that I was experiencing.

As the months and years after Don's death passed, I became more and more frustrated by my (perceived) inability to "deal" with this problem. By the time I arrived in Maine I was certain that I had experienced all the emotions associated with my loss, and that all remained for me was to have adequate time to "think about" things, and figure out what I needed to do to *solve this problem* once and for all.

What dawned on me that morning as I walked along the ocean was that the *last* thing I needed to do was to continue to "think about my problem". What I needed to do was accept the emotional component of this loss; the anger and resentment I felt about losing Don, the loneliness, the anxiety, the fear, the doubt, and the sense of failure I had about my reaction to the loss and the decisions I had made after his death.   I needed to stop thinking about my responses and emotions and see them for what they were, without judgment.

This is one of the great benefits of experiencing emotion during meditation; we practice (and it DOES take practice) by allowing ourselves to feel the emotions but not get attached to them.   By getting attached, I mean that we are thinking about how bad (or good) the emotions are making us feel, figuring out who (or what) is responsible for how we feel, and what we should do about it. So how do we *not* get attached?   I found that there were several components to non-attachment. The first was to recognize the emotion, whatever it is such as anger, sadness, longing. The second was to mentally "name" it – "This is anger", "This is sadness", "This is longing".   In naming the emotion, I found that I was consciously acknowledging its existence. The last component was to release it by mentally saying "I let go of my anger", "I let go of my sadness", "I let go of my longing". This does not mean that the feeling(s) wouldn't return again, it was likely that they would; maybe not now, but maybe tomorrow, or next week or next year. When they did I could repeat the steps described above.

This approach, of recognizing, naming, and releasing helped me to see the emotion in a non judgmental way, and perhaps more importantly prevented me from getting sidetracked with analyzing (why am I still having these feelings?), and berating (what is wrong with me, why can't I deal with this?) myself for the feelings as they occur. In other words less thinking, more acceptance.

These techniques can be applied outside the meditation session as well. With practice, identifying, naming, and releasing become habits. We find that our emotions become less toxic and hold less sway over how we react to them and, consequently, how we respond to emotionally charged situations. In time we can reap a beautiful by-product of this practice; compassion. First we experience compassion for ourselves when we stop beating ourselves up over what we feel

– guilt, regret, anger, hatred. Then we begin to develop compassion for others as we watch them struggle with their own emotional responses to life. By practicing non attachment to our emotional states, we also find ourselves attaching less to the emotional states and responses of the people around us. When we stop judging what we and others feel, our compassion and empathy can blossom and thrive.

TRAVELING LIGHT

I have been through several physical downsizings, and a few emotional ones too over the last 10 years. The first major (physical) one was when Don and I decided to sell our home and move into a condominium that was located on the top floor of a renovated silk mill. While the physical living space was only 100 square feet less than our former home, the storage space was considerably less – basically, we were losing a basement and a shed. Many of the items that were kept in the shed were things we wouldn't need in our new location, lawn mower, snow blower, garden tools. Living on the top floor meant no yard to take care of and living in the condo meant no snow to shovel , tasks that neither one of us were going to miss, especially the snow removal!

The second (and much more drastic) physical downsizing came when I decided to sell my home and move to Maine for a year. Not knowing where I would be living AFTER my time in Maine, I knew I needed to keep just enough "stuff" to furnish a studio or one bedroom apartment. I decided to downsize BEFORE moving because I wanted to be able to rent the smallest possible storage unit, AND I figured it was easier to divest myself of belongings before the move to Maine rather than after. While with family and friends I positioned the move as being only for a year, I really didn't know what I was going to be doing after that year was over; so ridding myself of "excess" felt like the right thing to do.

The decisions for this second downsizing were more intense. Which of Don's things did I keep? What trinkets and trifles that we had accumulated during our trips and time together did I hold on to? What did it say about me if I kept them or let them go? What did I do with the boxes of photographs, DVDs, CDs, and books? What did I do with the china (from my first marriage 30+ years before), that while beautiful didn't serve any useful purpose?

Thanks to technology, some of these decisions weren't as difficult as they might have been 10 years ago. Pictures were scanned and saved to CD's and flash drives, Music CD's were downloaded onto an iPod and then sold at my yard sale. Movies were culled through, some sold, while favorites were removed from their bulky cases and placed in a portable CD case. As for the more emotional items – I adopted a one box rule. One box of Christmas decorations, one box for mementos of Don, one box of trinkets. The rest were either given away or sold, including the china. This at times felt like a fairly ruthless process, but I kept myself focused on what my ultimate goals were in terms of space; as well as my evolving attitude toward "things".

My feelings toward "things" had been changing for some time. After my first marriage ended in divorce, I was still only in my mid-twenties. I spent the next 13 years single, moving around quite a bit and not making a whole lot of money; so my desire as well as my ability to accumulate "stuff" was limited. When I did finally decide on a career, and eventually

marriage to Don, success in both of these endeavors resulted in

a combination of feeling "settled" as well as having the financial

means to buy nice "stuff", new cars, travel, and well, you get

the idea.

I share this with you to let you know that I fit the pattern

of the prevailing American attitude. The "quality" and quantity

of your possessions and lifestyle reflected your success.   The

word "quality" in our culture is often confused with "cost", and

having finally tasted success in my chosen profession (success of

course being defined by job title and income), I was caught in

the cycle of work/spend, work/spend, work/spend.

The shift started to occur for me when I began to

experience burnout in my career. I had been working in the

Human Resources field for nearly 20 years, gradually assuming

positions with more and more responsibility.   The interesting

and rewarding part of that work for me (coaching, mentoring,

resolving problems, and building teams) had turned into

spending most of my time analyzing and reporting numbers and controlling costs.   By my mid forties, I was doing some soul searching.   I knew I was going to be working for another 15 – 20 years. Was THIS how I wanted to spend my time and energy?

Don and I spent many hours talking about what we wanted to do during the next phase of our lives.   He had been with the same company for many years and would be eligible to retire at age fifty-four. Both of us enjoyed helping people. After a lot of brain storming and discussion about the kind of life we wanted; we ended up agreeing that I would return to school to learn massage therapy and open up my own practice upon graduation.   Upon retirement, Don would also go to school and then join me in my practice.

This is an example of what I call "emotional downsizing".   When we experience a fundamental shift in what we perceive as important, in how we measure personal success, in how we define ourselves, we have achieved emotional downsizing.   Businesses call it a paradigm shift, Buddhists call it enlightenment.   It is different for everyone. The outcome isn't necessarily fiscal or physical austerity, but you will know what it is for you because the truth will resonate with you in some deep part of yourself. Soul, intuition, some release of chemicals in the brain – I won't pretend to know the "science" behind this shift, but you will recognize it when it happens.

By way of further defining this concept of emotional downsizing, let me share two other examples with you, in addition to my own.

The first story is about a woman I met when I was teenager.   My parents were very involved in their church. Since my brother and sister were older, and out on their own, we had empty bedrooms in our home which were often occupied by visiting missionaries, gospel singers, or just people struggling to get back on their feet. On one such occasion we had a Christian missionary who was living and working in Israel stay with us.   At the time of her visit to the USA this woman was nearly 80 years old. She had the energy, drive and spark of a person half her age. She also carried all of her earthly

possessions around in two suitcases. She owned one pair of

shoes. Her cherished possessions were a few small framed

photographs of family and a well worn bible. There were two

things (aside from her vivacious personality) that struck me.

The first was the obvious freedom that she felt at not being

constrained by owning a lot of stuff. Obviously, she had long

ago decided that what or how much she had in personal

possessions was not what defined who she was. Second, was

her complete and utter faith that what physical needs she did

have would be taken care of. Being of Christian faith she, of

course, believed that these needs were met by the God she

believed in (a philosophy that is not by the way limited to the

Christian belief system). Her non attachment to things

resonated with me on a deep level and left a lasting impression.

The second story involves friends of mine, a married

couple without children. They both have good jobs, they make

good money, and they live in a beautiful home and enjoy

traveling around the world. They also devote significant time and money to causes they believe in; take in foreign exchange students, and support their community in ways that are too numerous to mention (and besides it would embarrass them). They do not actively practice any religion, but have found the right balance of enjoying the "fruits of their labors" and sharing it with others, because doing so enriches their lives. In this case they do not do it because of any particular belief system, but simply because it resonates with them as the right thing to do.

So, call it what you will – enlightenment, emotional downsizing, paradigm shift; the examples I have shared with you are what I mean when I talk about traveling light. Traveling light can be about what we carry with us physically, but more often it is about what we carry with us emotionally, and how we decide to interact with the world around us.

For me, traveling light *did include* shedding possessions and reducing my income to live the kind of life I wanted. The first shift occurred in my mid-forties and was a joint decision made with my husband. It included shedding the perception that my success was defined by the amount of money I made. The second shift occurred after Don's death, and of course was far more impactful.

Along with Don's death came two financial surprises. The first was the insurance company, with whom we carried life insurance, denying payment because they said that Don's death occurred within the contestability period (within two years). The second was a misinterpretation of the monthly benefit I, as the surviving spouse, would be eligible for from Don's pension plan. This double blow coming on the heels of the sudden and shocking death of my husband left me reeling and feeling incredibly vulnerable about my financial security. There was still a mortgage and car payment to be made; and although my massage therapy practice was going well, I was only making a third of what I had been earning in my previous career. The knockout blow, financially, came a few months later when I tripped over an electrical cord and injured two fingers on my left hand; one was broken and the other severely sprained. Now my ability to practice massage was suspended for at least several months. By the time my fingers healed, I had neither the physical or emotional energy to jump start my practice. After all, part of "the plan" was for Don to join me in that practice in one capacity or another; and now that dream was shattered.

So, I was *forced* to process another physical AND emotional downsizing. I certainly wasn't feeling like this was an opportunity to become more enlightened. Far from it, I was seething with anger and resentment.

This brings me back to the physical downsizing that preceded my move to Maine. The act of shedding possessions, of picking and choosing, setting parameters for myself in terms of how much to keep was a necessary precursor in setting the stage for the emotional downsizing that I hoped was to follow. For me, a key ingredient was the feeling that I needed to "travel light". This was further emphasized by the fact that I was moving to a furnished 350 sq. ft. (think motel room with a kitchenette) apartment. Seven boxes of personal possessions were shipped in advance, and my car which was filled with two cats, a friend who served as my co-pilot for the 600 mile drive, and our luggage. This was the sum total of what I physically took to Maine.

Frankly, at this point I was eager for this temporary (or maybe permanent) *unloading* of "stuff". I was going to Maine for the purpose of answering questions such as: What is precious to me, what defines me, and who am I?

Fortunately, I was able to find answers to those questions and more. If you are dealing with loss, I encourage you to look at the loss you are struggling with as a chance to answer these questions for yourself. It's a horrible way to have to search for answers, and any one of us would certainly choose an easier path, but that isn't the hand we've been dealt. Loss, especially profound loss, places us in the position of being able to define who we are and what is important to us in ways that people who have not yet experienced such loss cannot. I say, "yet", because sooner or later everyone will experience loss.

When you do find *your* answers, I guarantee that you will recognize them when you find them, for you will feel a shift occur deep inside of you. You will be able to better cope with your loss and make better decisions about how to react to it. Your answers may or may not include physically reducing your belongings. For me, that was (and continues to be) a critical part of how I want to live. I simply don't want to drag a lot of "stuff" around. I want to be light and nimble; both mentally and physically. Having less, reducing my consumption, repurposing, these are guiding principles and part of what defines me at this point in my life. Not having to spend time (and money) on acquiring and maintaining possessions allows me to spend my energy on answering the questions "What Kind of Life Do I Want", and engaging in the actions and behaviors that will get me there.

If you choose to pursue what it means to "Travel Light",

I wish you well on your journey and hope that the sharing my

own experience is of value to you in some way.

ON BEING AWAKE

"Here it is – right now.   Start thinking about it and you miss it."
Huang-po

Someone once asked the Buddha how he wanted to be remembered.   He answered simply: "Remember me as the one who woke up".   Of course Buddha was referring to enlightenment, more specifically the Four Noble Truths, the Eightfold Path, and the vast array of other teachings that have evolved to become Buddhism in the various forms that are practiced today.

Why is "waking up" so hard to do, and why does it often take the death of a loved one or some other type of significant loss to force us to wake up?   I have discussed some of the reasons I think prevent us from living an "awake" life in other essays, but I will summarize them here.

- Thinking we have control over our lives and destiny (The Control Illusion/Delusion)
- Refusal to accept that life is suffering (Dukka Happens)

- Refusal to let go of our attachments (to people, relationships, emotions, things)

- Ego (belief that we are right, that we deserve happiness, that we are special)

- Immersion in, and distraction with, our way of life (acquisition, media, chemicals, habits, rituals, "busyness")

- Clinging to the past or focusing on the future rather than being in the moment (Be Here Now)

We humans believe ourselves to be "evolved" in our thinking and yet not much has changed over the course of mankind's history.   From a technological standpoint we have evolved, and we have become "smarter" over the centuries (thanks to the mental accomplishments of a relatively small number of human minds) but emotionally we remain unchanged.   We are still ruled by primal instincts, such as the fight or flight response.   We continue to experience the same emotions, and act and react in the same way that our ancestors have acted and reacted for thousands of years.

In order to wake up, we need to change the way we view the world and our interaction with it. We need to develop what the Zen Buddhists call "Beginner's mind".   It refers to having an attitude of openness and eagerness toward all things. In the beginner's mind there are many possibilities. Another term that is commonly used is "Don't Know Mind", which means essentially the same thing – we approach all things (interactions, relationships, situations) with the spirit of "I don't know", assuming nothing.

Early in my career, the company I worked for was making a sincere attempt to engage employees at all levels of the organization in becoming stakeholders in our success. It was a small manufacturing facility, employing approximately 300 people. It was the late 1980's when employee involvement, ESOPS (employee stock ownership plans), and upside down management were in vogue.   Our strategy to promote employee involvement was to institute a creative problem solving process called "Simplex"©.   Many years later I still find this process to be one of the most effective tools available as a way to promote creativity and participation in solving problems and making decisions.   I use it (or parts of it) all the time in my own decision making.

The key step throughout the Simplex © process is the separation of divergent and convergent thinking. Divergent thinking is when we set aside our logic, judgment, and assumptions (such as saying: "that will never work"), but instead consider all possibilities in developing solutions or making decisions. Convergent thinking is when we bring our logic and judgment back into the process.   Convergent thinking tools include research, analysis, and weighing the probable outcome and success of various solutions.   Both types of thinking are necessary to the problem solving process; the *key* is learning to separate the two.

Divergent thinking is a contemporary example of having beginner's mind. When we set aside our logic and judgment, we consider all possibilities. We approach the problem or the situation with an open mind. We set aside our assumptions about why someone is behaving a certain way. We stop analyzing why something happened the way it did, or stop expecting a certain outcome.   We don't assume that we know the "right" answer, or that we have the market cornered on "the way things should be". The reason this process works so beautifully in the business world is because it creates a level playing field when you bring together people from different "hierarchies" in the organization. If everyone is following the process (which is run by a trained facilitator) all ideas and opinions are equally valued.

In order to successfully apply beginner's mind, don't know mind, or divergent thinking in our own lives we must be willing to set aside our ego. It is ego that demands we always be right, demands that we be heard, and demands that we get our own way. When we stop feeding the ego, we can relax and allow ourselves to be open to all possibilities. We free ourselves from expecting a certain result, and remove self- imposed limits on our thinking and actions. In other words, we can wake up.

A significant loss in our lives creates (whether we want it to or not) an environment for waking up, because loss has a way of stripping away long held assumptions about the way things "should be". We are forced to face a new reality and truth as a result of the loss. It is a paradigm shift of momentous proportions.

But even though our "awakening" can be a rude one, we have a choice whether or not to embrace that new reality. By that I don't mean to suggest that you should rejoice in your loss. What I mean is that by applying the principles of beginner's mind to our new reality we can approach the changes with a different attitude.   The first step is to accept that we, like everyone else, are going to experience suffering. Once we get over that hurdle, we can use beginner's mind to face what comes next. As we deal with the loss we can practice setting aside our judgment about how others may react to our loss, or the decisions we make in order to move forward. More importantly, we can practice setting aside judgment of *ourselves.*

Being awake and living with beginner's mind doesn't mean that you blissfully go through life with a "what will be will be" attitude. If you go back to my original definition of beginner's mind, I talk about being open and being eager. This requires a certain degree of alertness. When we practice beginner's mind we remain alert to *all* the possibilities set before us. For example, I enjoy driving around and exploring back roads, and I have a decent sense of direction. Nothing gives me more satisfaction then finding a "short cut", or a new and different way to get from point A to point B. This process does not involve using a GPS unit. It may mean having a map or compass for back up, but it is much more satisfying to figure it out on my own. The process of exploring these back roads requires me to be open to all options. Should I turn left or right at this crossroads? Should I go straight or turn around? It requires me to remain alert. Do I recognize that road name? Did I just pass a route sign or town indicator? This process of exploring also requires me to be open to the possibility of failure. I may not find a better route, or I may get 25 miles off track and have to drive further and longer than I expected. It means I may have to admit defeat.

Being awake and using beginner's mind is simple, but it is not easy. It requires effort, it requires taking a step back from our emotions, and it requires letting go of our expectations. It is going to bed with the realization that you didn't do so well at being "awake" today, but tomorrow you will try again. It means not giving up. The beauty of awakening is that although it *can* be an "aha" type of experience, more often than not it is a gradual process. It is two steps forward and one step back.

Being awake is all about possibility. There is the possibility of joy; there is the possibility of sorrow. There is the possibility

153

of success, and the possibility of disappointment. There is the possibility of finding our way or of losing it. If we remain alert, if we are open and eager to experiencing the outcomes, whatever they may be, they will be easier to accept because we are approaching them without expectation. We accept them because we realize that the outcomes do not define us. They do not *mean* anything, they are what they are, and the next phase of our life or the next similar situation will likely be a completely different experience or yield a totally different result.

What comes next? I don't know. But whatever it is, I will be okay. I'm just waking up.

FINDING MY TRIBE

"When there is no place that you have decided to call your own, then no matter where you go, you are always heading home".

Muso Soseki

Most of us want to feel like we "belong" to something. Why else would we get involved in various organizations, churches, or groups? We do it so we don't feel so alone. We do it so we are surrounded by others, who share common interests, believe the things we believe, or live the same lifestyle we live. This is reflected (often) by our physical surroundings. The neighborhood we live in, the kind of car we drive, the clothes we wear, and the technology we carry. These are cues to the people around us that we are like *them,* that we are members of the same tribe. Associating with people who are similar to us in socio-economic status, thinking, and beliefs serves as positive reinforcement for us on a daily basis. I'm okay, I am liked, I am normal, I *belong.* When I use the term "tribe" here I am really referring to the multiple tribes to which we belong. Unlike earlier cultures where the tribe encompassed every aspect of their members lives; in today's society we may be members of many tribes – family, friends, co-workers, school, organizations, and so on.   To keep it simple, I am grouping them all together under the umbrella term "tribe".

After a loss, that sense of security about belonging is often questioned, if not completely shattered. Old friends disappear, either because you no longer fit their profile of what they think their tribe is, or because they are afraid to be confronted with the emotional aspects of your loss.   It embarrasses them, they don't know what to say, or they are afraid it could happen to them.   Your own sense about what is important also changes after a loss; your emotional state may be such that you just don't *feel* like participating in the tribe's activities, or your financial status may be such that you can no longer afford the tribe's activities.

In time you may find that you go back to the tribe and resume your involvement as it was before. However, many people who have suffered a loss, especially those such as death of a spouse or young child, divorce, and financial loss find their tribe has been altered permanently. This is a type of "secondary loss"; meaning changes that occur in your relationships, employment, or home as a result of the initial loss. You will feel grief over these secondary losses too, although the lines between grief for the initial loss and grief for the secondary loss may be blurred.

You are likely to feel lonely and isolated. The death of a spouse or partner means that every aspect of your daily life and routine is altered. For example, my husband and I shared the household responsibilities equally. When he died, I had to begin doing the grocery shopping (a job I hated), cleaning the litter boxes, and taking out the trash among other things. I no longer had to clean the spilt coffee grounds every morning, or rinse out the large salad bowl that always made it to the sink, but never the dishwasher. How I missed those tasks when he was gone! These same alterations take place when you lose a spouse through divorce; even a separation that you may have wanted. In the case of job loss, your routine is altered by not having to be at a certain place at a certain time, and not seeing your co-workers on a daily basis. These changes extend to your social interactions as well. In the loss of a child, all the connections you may have had through his or her activities are gone, so the nature of your interaction with those people is altered. As a result your tribe is changed.

You may be surprised by how much this change affects your self esteem. Before Don's death I considered myself a confident person, self reliant, secure in my tribe. After his death those feelings of isolation began to chip away at my self esteem. I felt so broken inside that I did not see how it was possible to be attractive to anyone, and I don't mean this solely from a romantic standpoint. I did not feel that I had anything to offer as a friend, relative, or employee let alone a romantic interest! This is just another example of how a loss changes *everything.*

I did get a lot of support from my tribe after Don's death. But the tribe did change. Some changed because, at the time of my loss, I had neither the energy nor desire to maintain my role in the tribe; and by the time I did have my energy or desire back, the tribe had moved on without me. Some changed because I no longer fit the tribe's "profile". Some changed because my new circumstances made them uncomfortable. Some changed because being with them was too painful a reminder to me of my old life, and I let them slip away. So I know that if you are reading this, you are likely experiencing similar changes in your own tribe. You need to be prepared that your tribe members are not going to alter their lives, routines and patterns to accommodate your changed circumstances. Early after the loss, yes, they will. They will bring you food, they will visit, they will invite you out; but as time goes by they will slip back into their "normal" routine long before you have established a new "normal" for yourself.

Rather than sitting around and moping about how your tribe is changing, I encourage you to use this as an opportunity to ask yourself what does it mean to "belong"?   What is important to you? Did you consciously choose the tribe you were in before the loss occurred, or did the tribe just evolve out of work, family, in-laws, your spouse's friends, your child's activities? Did you really *want* these people in your tribe anyway?! Don't misunderstand me; I'm not suggesting that you toss aside your whole "tribe" after a loss. I'm only suggesting that it is natural for your tribe to change as a result of your loss, and when it does, it is an opportunity to re-evaluate what tribe(s) you want to join and who will be in your tribe. Kind of like the TV show "Survivor".

When I moved to Maine, I left my old tribe behind geographically. I didn't know anyone in Bar Harbor. I had some ideas about how I would meet people, but I certainly didn't know if those ideas would lead to new friends. Having lived in the same geographic area for most of my life, I was fairly dependant on my old tribe for my social interactions, and I was resistant to cultivating new ones. However, I couldn't expect my old tribe to adapt to my circumstances. I was the one that had to adapt and create my own new normal. So when I moved to Maine I approached people with the same spirit I approached the relocation itself. "I am open". I am open to whomever I meet and what they have to teach me. Because no one knew me, they had no preconceived idea about who I was before Don died, what my life was like, how much money I had, or how his death had changed me. And I had no preconceived idea of them. This turned out to be a beautiful and rewarding experience, and when I left Maine, I left behind an interesting mix of new friends; very different from the tribe I had back in Pennsylvania.

My experience in Maine taught me some important lessons:

1. Everyone has something to offer.

2. When you extend acceptance without judgment you are more likely to get acceptance without judgment in return.

3. Everyone has experienced or is experienced suffering, we are all so very alike. Recognizing this allows compassion to flow from us. Compassion creates bridges, bridges we can cross to meet new friends.

4. Home is not where you come from, but where you are. Not that you forget your "old tribe", but you enjoy the moment you are in with your new tribe.

5. "Belonging" is an illusion. When we set aside the ego and our need to impress, our need to be liked, our need to "belong", we can interact with people in a more authentic way.

So treasure your tribe, but realize as with all things, our tribes are temporary; they will change as we change. Recognizing this we can move through life as the beautiful quote at the beginning of this piece states. With an open heart and an open mind toward ourselves and others; we are

always heading home and we can always find a tribe.

WHAT IS ESSENTIAL IS INVISIBLE TO THE "I"

"It is only with the heart that one can see rightly. What is essential is invisible to the eye."

Antoine de Saint-Exupery

I took some liberty in the title of this essay with a play on words – "I" exchanged for "eye". The book from which this title is cannibalized is "The Little Prince" by Antoine de Saint-Expury. A beautiful fable written in 1943; I have found it to contain some profound truths about human nature and what is important. It is a book that should be digested slowly, like a fine meal, taken in small bites, and savored at length. I like to pull it out and read it every few years, and with each reading I discover some new wisdom.

Perhaps my favorite section in the book is the story of the Little Prince and his encounter with a fox. The fox asks the boy to "tame" him, and the author goes on to beautifully describe the process of how these two characters become friends. The fox asks to be "tamed" even though he knows that the boy must someday leave him. When the boy goes to leave, the fox begins to cry, and the boy is sad that he has hurt the fox's feelings. But the fox explains that it is worth suffering the sadness, because the color of the golden wheat in the field will remind him of the color of the boy's hair, and he will have that happy memory to carry with him when the boy is gone. The fox then goes on to share a secret with the boy of how when we "tame" something it becomes unique to us "in all the world"; because of the relationship we share with that person or thing. While no one else may notice or understand it, to us it will be special.......and so the secret the fox shares with the boy is that "what is essential is invisible to the eye".

I discovered this story many years before I experienced the death of my husband, but as I read it now and consider it in the context of loss, I am struck with how the author is actually describing the law of impermanence, and that the act of loving someone will inevitably cause us sorrow because everything changes. What is beautiful about this particular story is that the fox enters the relationship with the full knowledge that he will suffer the loss of his friend at some point.   This only serves to make the time they have together that much more precious, as the fox discovers a way to take an everyday ordinary thing (the color of the wheat), as a way to remember his time with the boy.   In the end, the fox loses the boy (as the boy continues on his travels), but because the fox understands that all things are temporary, he is able to let the boy go, therefore, minimizing the suffering for both of them.

It is our selfish ego that restricts our ability to let go of our attachment to people and things, along with our expectations of them; but once we grasp that the nature of *everything* is impermanent, we are ready to take that next giant step and realize that this impermanent nature also applies to us!   I say this is a giant step, because everything about our society denies that this (our impermanent nature) is so. We are bombarded with messages starting in childhood about the importance of achievement, the importance of striving, and the importance of making "a contribution".   We are surrounded by a culture that is obsessed with youth.   When we become seriously ill or old, we are compelled to seek "health" and delay death for as long as possible.   We are barraged with illusions of beauty and perfection which not only create an impossible expectation but one that also desensitizes us to the suffering of others.   We are shocked when confronted with horrific acts on the part of nature and mankind that cause suffering for others, because we have done everything we can to keep the reality that life is suffering at a distance.   We search for explanations (scientific or divine), or blame the victims as ways to rationalize our unwillingness to accept these two basic truths.

But if we are willing to cut through all the illusions, the smoke and mirrors that we and our society have created, we are able to grasp that our nature, as well as the nature of every other animate and inanimate creature and thing, is one of impermanence.   This is the concept that the Buddhists refer to as "no self". And with this newfound awareness we should not feel frightened, but free.   We can be free to more fully

appreciate every person that we encounter.   We can be free to

cherish every interaction we have.   We can be free from

getting bogged down in petty disagreements with our family,

friends, and co-workers. We can be free to approach people

and opportunities with curiosity and enthusiasm; and most

importantly, we can be free to detach from our ego.

Some people think that if they embrace the concept of

"no self" and that "our nature is impermanent", then nothing

matters; that we can do whatever we want.   In fact, the

opposite is true – *everything matters*.   Everything takes on

new significance and importance when we realize that what we

are experiencing in each moment may never happen again.   It

strips away the assumption that things will be tomorrow as they

are today, that we will have another opportunity to say "thank

you", or "I love you", or "I'm sorry".

Some people argue that if the nature of everything is

impermanent, then why would I want to expose myself to

suffering by falling in love, making friends, having children? The answer to that is simple. You are going to have suffering regardless, because life is suffering. If you choose not be vulnerable, not to be involved with others, then you will suffer the feelings of loneliness and isolation. Why not choose to experience the joy of bringing someone else happiness, of making someone smile, or of holding the hand of another who is suffering. We do it because, as the fox says to the boy, "of the color of the wheat fields".

I also think we choose to be vulnerable *because* of our nature, for the law of impermanence is also one of connectedness. Nothing exists in isolation. The computer I am typing on exists because of the collective efforts of many people; from the designers and the programmers, to the assemblers and packagers, to the person who delivered it to my door.

What is essential is invisible to the "I". In letting go of our egos, we can realize the truth of this statement. We can embrace our nature and choose connection. I leave you with

one last thought; one of my favorite Buddhist "prayers".

"And let me respectfully remind you

that life and death are of supreme importance.

Time swiftly passes by and opportunity is lost.

Each of us should strive to awaken.

Awaken!

Take heed – do not squander your life."

I REALLY SHOULD.....

One of my objectives in moving to Maine was to better understand how the negative aspects of my thinking were hindering my recovery.   It wasn't long before I zeroed in on how often my thinking was dominated by the word "Should". I don't know that experiencing a loss makes me any different from the rest of humanity in that regard. However, I have *come* to realize just how much emotional anxiety and suffering this type of thinking causes. Here is a list of my most common "shoulds" from the last few years:

- I should work out more

- I should diet

- I should visit my parents more often

- I should have a vegetable garden

- I should do "xyz" to the house

- I should go out more, make new friends

- I should stop grieving

- I should go back into a management job

- ·I should stop eating " xyz"

- I should stop worrying about the future

- I should take a class in "xyz"

- I should learn to relax

And the list goes on. Sound familiar?

An exercise I have found to be most helpful, is to turn these "Shoulds" into "Wants". Now "want" can be a dangerous word too, because "want" can very quickly turn into "expectation and desire", which is just one short step away from attachment and WHAM, you are right back into creating suffering for yourself.   So I will tread carefully into this minefield of the using the word "want".

When I catch myself hearing the word "should" too much, I turn it into a question. For example when I hear "I should work out more/exercise more" (a pretty common one); I rephrase it to "Why do I think I should work out/exercise more?" Answer: "I want to be strong enough to hike

172

mountains; doing this will help me maintain and build my health; doing this will help me achieve my goal of walking 1000 miles this year."

I find that when I change the internal dialogue from thinking about what I "should" be doing into a positive dialogue that is based on WHY I want to be doing certain things, it helps me to identify and separate the positives from the negatives. Also, thinking in terms of "should" creates negative expectations of me, because when I don't do what I think I "should", then I feel like a failure.

I also find that it is important that I be compassionate with myself. Most of us tend to be very compassionate and understanding of others and their struggles, but much less so when it comes to ourselves. So what are some ways in which I practice this act of self compassion?

- I try to be realistic: I accept that I am not going to do the best thing for myself every day, all day. I am human, and therefore, imperfect.

- I try to let go of expectations: There are many things you cannot control (ok, most things actually), but there are a few that you can control. Going back to my example of working out: as a person who deals with an auto-immune problem, I know that there are going to be some days when I am too tired or in too much pain to accomplish much in the way of exercise. I will never be able to exercise at the same level as someone who does not have the condition I have. To think this would be creating an unrealistic expectation. When I let go of this expectation, I am much more likely to focus on that which I CAN accomplish versus what I cannot. Unrealistic expectations, much like "shoulds", are de-motivating. On the other hand, realistic goals and defining WHY we WANT to do something is much more likely to move us forward in a positive direction.

- I try to let go of others' expectations of me: A wise person once said "You can please some of the people some of the time, but you can't please all of the people all of the time". And of course we all have people in our lives that we will never please no matter what we do! These people create wonderful opportunities for us to learn about the power "I should" has in our lives, and the impact of the expectations we create for ourselves as a result. For that is exactly what they are, created expectations. The expectation may have been created by someone else, but the choice of whether or not to accept it lies with us. The key here is to look at responsibility versus choice. Asking ourselves, "what is my **responsibility** in this situation is far more empowering (and positive) then saying "I will **never** please this person", thus getting caught up in a frustrating loop of negative reinforcement. We can then **choose** to accept the responsibility in the situation, but choose NOT to accept the expectation. There is a difference!

- I accept that I am not always going to get what I want: This is akin to letting go of expectations. Life is full of compromises. We all have limitations on ourselves; through choices we've made, genetics and circumstances. Life requires adaptation; we need only to look at nature to see this. When this occurs, I ask myself, "How can I adapt what I want to the situation I am in?" The answer to this question usually translates into identifying an action I can take that is appropriate to the situation. The sooner we learn how to adapt to our ever-changing environment, the less frustration we will have because we will be focusing on what we *can* do versus getting caught up in wishing the situation were different so we can have what we "want".

When you find yourself in a slump of negative feelings and emotions, may I suggest that you need only look at how many times a day you are using the word "should" to see that you are creating your own negative reality.   However, with time, practice, and self compassion, you CAN learn to change and adapt.

THE FINE ART OF DOING NOTHING

"For who knows where the time goes?"
                                    Sandy Denny

I sometimes think that I may be inherently lazy.   Not lazy in the sense that I procrastinate or that I lack motivation, but lazy in the sense that I can be very comfortable just hanging out; gazing out the window, sitting on a park bench, or sipping a cup of tea.   I suppose this comes with being a "day dreamer". One of my teachers actually wrote in my high school yearbook: "keep daydreaming, it's good for you".   Apparently, this was a skill that came to me naturally even at a young age.

Lazy seems like such a negative term, so I prefer to think of it as being skilled at the fine art of doing nothing. Doing nothing correctly is more difficult than it sounds. We are so programmed to believe that we need to be accomplishing something with every moment of our day, that we feel guilty when we stop.   Many of us also don't like the thoughts we

have when we do nothing, so it is easier to hold them at bay

by keeping ourselves busy and distracted.   I'm not sure when it

became so terrifying to "be alone with our thoughts", but our

culture bombards us with the idea that it is bad to be alone, bad

to be still, bad to be doing nothing.   The average American

spends 6 – 8 hours a day watching television which deceives us

into thinking we are doing "something"; but this is an example

of *really* doing nothing.   I say this not to denigrate watching

television.   I do it from time to time when I am living

somewhere that I actually *have* television; but television is an

example of a passive form of doing nothing, with neither brain

nor body engaged.

The kind of doing nothing that I'm talking about is a

more active form.   It is more mindful then it is mindless.   It is

doing nothing *with intention.*   What I mean by that is that we

make a conscious choice to just be still, to just be with our

thoughts.   It can be similar to meditation if we choose it to be, by letting our thoughts come and go like a gentle breeze, or it can be engaging as in a pleasant daydream such as thinking about places we would like to visit, meeting a favorite musician or author, or imagining what kind of work or business we would like to do.   For example, when I see a house that I like, I imagine what the inside of the house looks like, what colors the walls are, what kind of furniture they have, what the views are from various windows.   Another example is taking a favorite movie character and expanding on their story.   Creating new stories out of the one that has been presented to me. (Reading this I think perhaps I should take up fiction writing after all!)   I also enjoy hiking to a favorite overlook, then sitting for 20 minutes to just enjoy the view.   For me this often means being next to water, watching the birds, boats, and waves.

I also believe that "doing nothing" is good for you, both mentally and physically.   Major religious practices encourage this. For example many Christians declare Sunday as "a day of rest".   Jews observe the Sabbath (which prohibits certain activities during this time). I believe there is wisdom in this. I can't help but wonder if many of the maladies that our culture suffers from, such as depression, fibromyalgia, and chronic fatigue, can be tied back to the fact that we have distracted and "busied" ourselves to the point of mental and physical exhaustion. I do not mean to suggest that this is the *sole* cause for these illnesses; I'm merely speculating on busyness as a contributing factor. I **would** argue that ignoring our need to be still, to be silent, at the very least deprives us of so many wonderful opportunities to just be present in the moment and appreciate that place in time for what it is.

As with all things, balance is essential. We can very quickly get *too* good at the fine art of doing nothing. If you find yourself spending all of your spare time doing nothing, or neglecting the things that need to get done because you are doing nothing, then chances are your "doing nothing" time is really just "wasting time", and there is a difference. Doing nothing time should refresh your spirit, improve your mood, and motivate subsequent action. If it doesn't, if you feel bored, sluggish, or frustrated with yourself; then probably you *are* just wasting time.

That is why I refer to doing nothing as an art. I approach it several ways. Sometimes it is a reward. When my work is done, when my chores are completed, when I have exercised, then I get to visit one of my favorite overlooks, or sit in my favorite chair. Other times it is catalyst, done early in the day with a cup of tea in a quiet spot. So indulged, my mind and body are then ready to begin the work of the day. Sometimes, I use it as a break; if the work is not going well, or I am feeling frustrated and stressed, I stop, change the scenery and give my brain time to relax and unwind. Refreshed, I can then resume whatever I am doing with renewed interest and attention. Sometimes my doing nothing time is 10 minutes, sometimes an hour. More time then this I, either rarely have, or for me it turns into wasting time.

You can easily incorporate doing nothing into other activities. If you like to walk, find a bench or tree log to stop at and sit for 10 minutes before continuing on your way. If you go to the gym, relax in the steam room or sauna, if they have one, or sit by the pool. If you enjoy a cocktail after work, instead of turning on the TV, sit quietly with your drink in a favorite chair and gaze out the window or go sit outside. Likewise, at the start of your day enjoy your coffee or tea without the noise of the radio or television. If your house is full of people, retreat for 15 minutes to your bedroom or home office. Better yet, encourage the entire household to practice the fine art of doing nothing for 10 minutes between school and dinner. The world won't end, and your family won't starve if dinner is served 10 or 15 minutes later than usual. With practice you will find that you can shut out the noise around you and enjoy doing nothing even in the busiest of places such as airports, parks, and shopping malls.

I find that when I allow myself to have these times of doing nothing my attention and focus is better, I sleep better, and I respond better to stress.   Doing nothing is a kindness you can do for yourself, which will benefit not only you, but the people around you.   What could be nicer than to have someone ask "What are you doing", and you respond by saying: "Nothing".

BE HERE NOW

"When human conversation stops, the world is anything but quiet". Barbara Kingsolver, Prodigal Summer

As someone who was constantly thinking about the future and planning ahead, the practice of "being in the now" did not come easily to me.   Even as a young person I had a tendency to be thinking about what I wanted to accomplish, where I wanted to live, how I wanted my house to look, and what kind of car I wanted to drive.   When my career led me into a management position, a great deal of my time was spent in anticipating problems and planning for the future through budgeting, analysis, and projections.   Heading off problems before they occurred was a big part of my success in business. So it was only natural for me to continue this kind of thinking in my life outside of work too.   I would describe it as being more of a habit then an obsession.   Besides, it was always good to have something to look forward to – the next vacation, the next ice hockey season, the next week-end, the next holiday, the next..........whatever.   When I changed careers and opened up my own business, this habit of thinking about the future continued to provide enjoyment.   How would I grow my business, where would I be in three years, five years?

Despite my "addiction" to thinking about the future, there was a part of me that realized that in spending so much time "living forward" I was missing the present moment.   I had been reading about "being in the moment" and felt that this was a new habit that I wanted to cultivate in my life.   When I became a massage therapist, I found that in order for my clients to receive the best possible massage, I needed to be completely in the moment; concentrating on finding the tension in their bodies, identifying which muscles needed to be stretched, and listening to what their words were really conveying about their physical state.   This was very different from my previous work experience, in which I had to constantly balance and shift my focus back and forth between the present and future.   In the therapeutic setting, it was critical that for that hour long session I be totally present with the client and in what I was doing. It was in this environment that I began to fully grasp the importance of "being in the moment".

When Don died I was left with an uncertain and undesirable future. The formerly pleasurable and rewarding activity of thinking ahead and planning for the future became a nightmarish exercise that created in me fear and panic. Thinking about the present wasn't so great either, and thinking about the past only left me feeling sad and longing to have back what I had lost. So I tried not to think at all. I watched movies, read books, did puzzles, slept; anything to distract me from having to think about the reality of my new life as a widow.

Gradually, I began to accept my present reality, but I didn't like it much, and thinking about the future seemed pointless. This was not a very peaceful place in which to dwell mentally or physically, but what were my options? Obviously, there was no going back. I had no hope for my future, and I felt stuck in an unsatisfying present. It was like walking in place or driving with one foot on the gas and the other foot on the

brake; going nowhere.

My decision to move to Maine, specifically Mount

Dessert Island, was in many ways, an act of desperation.

Acadia and the island had for years been my place of retreat

and sanctuary. It was as I like to say: "the second great love of

my life". No place or person (other than Don) had given me

the same sense of serenity that Acadia National Park did.   I felt

that if I were to ever attain a sense of peace about my current

life and regain a sense of hope for my future, it would happen

there.

As soon as I crossed the narrows that separate the

mainland from the island, a sense of relief and anticipation

swept over me.   I felt relief at being in a place of such beauty

and peace, and anticipation for the time I was about to spend

there and what I might learn.

When I walked the carriage roads and hiked the trails, I

was finally able to begin slowing down my anxious mind. "Be

Here Now" became my mantra. When I felt my thoughts

heading down the road of worry about the future or longing for

the past, I would pull on my hiking boots and get out into the

park. There I was able to engage my senses in the moment. I

filled myself with the sight of the water, the color of trees, the

texture of the bark, and the smell of balsam pine and salt air. I

heard only the sound of the waves, the wind and seagulls.

Being in a place that I loved so much helped me to bring myself

into the present, wonderful moment.   The only thing that I

needed to accomplish right then and there was to be living in

that moment and no other.   I learned to appreciate the

nuances of the park during all seasons – biting cold, fresh snow,

budding trees, changing tides, driving rain, crashing surf, lakes

as smooth as glass, falling leaves, fog shrouded mountains; each

moment was unique, each moment a new experience to be

savored, each moment becoming precious in the knowledge

that it would not come again.

With practice, I was able to begin applying "Be Here Now" to other more ordinary moments. Activities such as washing the dishes, putting away library books, walking my cat, and driving to work could be equally engrossing. Naturally, this required a bit more concentration, because not all of those activities were as pleasurable or satisfying as walking in the park; but they became just as meaningful.

I learned that being in the moment, aside from helping me not to obsess and worry about what the future held; also released me from expectations about what I thought "should" be happening in the present. For example, when you live along the coast of the North Atlantic the weather can change pretty quickly. You could begin your walk under a cloudless sky and an hour later the sky would be completely overcast. You could leave your home in snow and reach your destination in rain. You could look out to a sun- filled sky, drive ten miles and be enveloped by fog. That type of environment teaches you two things: Don't expect anything, and be prepared for everything.   So why worry about what is going to happen? Just take it as it comes, enjoy it for what it is, then let it go and move on to the next moment.

Of course it is unrealistic to think that we can live our lives never thinking about the future. There are appointments to schedule, commitments to be kept, birthdays to celebrate, and bills to be paid. What being in the moment is *really* about is not ignoring the future, but rather not worrying about it, or more importantly, attaching an expectation of what could or "should" happen. Researchers say that this is one of the reasons so many people feel a letdown after the December holidays. We put so much time, energy, and money into preparing for the festivities that we create an unrealistic expectation of what they "should" be like. We expect the food to turn out perfectly, we expect children to "come home", and we expect gifts to be appreciated. We set ourselves up for failure and disappointment again and again. How much more would we enjoy the holiday if we let go of our expectations and just appreciated the time for whatever it brought?   Accept

today for what it is, for to anticipate tomorrow is an exercise in

futility as it has not yet come.

"Be Here Now" is a constant application of effort.

Some days are easier than others.   But the reward is worth the

effort.   Several months into my year in Maine I wrote these

words down in my journal and I'd like to share them with you

now.

"Let go of the irretrievable past,

Let go of the unpredictable future,

And discover yourself,

Living in the present".

EMPTY ME

When everything is empty, there can be no attachment.

Note from my journal

I am going to commit either an act of extreme bravery or an act of extreme foolishness by attempting to explain the Buddhist concept of "emptiness", and talk about how it relates to loss.

The first thing that we, as westerners, must do is set aside our thinking that empty and emptiness are negatives. To the western way of thinking when something is "empty" it is the same as "nothing". We say, especially after suffering a loss that we "feel empty inside". This is, in our minds a bad thing, a negative feeling. A popular pop psychology exercise is to ask someone how they view a glass of liquid filled halfway. Is the glass half empty or is the glass half full? What is implied is that if you view the glass as being half full you are a positive thinker but if you view the glass as being half empty you are a negative thinker.

To the Buddhist, everything is empty.   For them to understand and embrace this concept is a beautiful thing because it means that they have liberated themselves from attachment and fully grasped the concept of impermanence.

In the essay "Who Am I", I talked about how we use labels to define ourselves.   This use of labels extends to our entire universe.   This is a chair, this is a teapot, and this is a cat. We then use these labels to assign value to something (or someone), determine characteristics, and associate it with an emotion; such as this is a hard (or soft) chair, this is a hot (or cool), teapot, this is a sweet (or mean) cat.

Labels and their associated connotations are how we communicate with one another.   But to someone who has never seen a chair, or touched a teapot, or interacted with a cat, these labels mean nothing, they are just empty words. The labels we use and the feelings we associate with them are how we form attachments.   This is my cat, these are my shoes, this is my smart phone, this is my house, this is my car, this is my child, my wife and so on.   Notice a pattern?   Me, my, mine. On occasion, we become generous and use the word "our", such as this is our house, our company, our children.   But nine times out of ten it is "me, my, mine".   And, bingo (!), attachment.

Attachments in and of themselves are not bad things. Attachments can lead to making a commitment to a person or a cause, motivate us to complete a project or get a degree, and bring us moments of happiness and pleasure.   However, attachments have a tendency to create expectations.   We expect that someone will always love us. We expect that if we get a certain degree we will find a job making "X" number of dollars. We expect that we will always be able to afford or be physically capable of doing a certain activity.   And of course we have the biggest expectation of them all – that life will remain the same.

As I have discussed in other essays, the expectation that things will remain the same is simply not a realistic one. Nothing can remain the same when impermanence is a universal law. However, instead of accepting that everything is impermanent, we work and strive, plead and bargain (with others, with "God", with the Universe) to make this not so. These actions serve only to make matters worse for us when the inevitable changes do occur.

This brings me back to emptiness. If everything is impermanent, therefore, everything must be empty. By empty, I mean that everything is made up of temporary, impermanent parts. Everything has a life cycle, an expiration date. Our bodies are made up of thousands of working parts; some of those parts last longer than others. A television is made up of hundreds of parts that must be assembled in a certain way in order for the television to work, and as in our bodies these parts wear out at different rates. A hardwood chair is made up of wood and glue. Depending on the quality of these substances and the quality of the workmanship, a chair may last 5 years or 50 years. The chair's life cycle can be affected by the elements it is exposed to, the number and size of the people that sit on it, and how it is treated. We can extend the life cycle of the chair by how we take care of it, but a tornado, fire or flood could come along and ruin the chair regardless of how much care we took. It is that "law of impermanence" and uncertainty that reveals the reality that everything is "empty". This is why this concept of emptiness is an important one to grasp. Regardless of the labels we attach, everything is impermanent, and therefore, empty. The idea that anything in life remains the same, whether it is a person, a pet, a job, a relationship, a car, or a favorite fishing spot, is an illusion. By understanding that everything is empty, we can still appreciate and enjoy what we have in our lives while those things are here, but accept that they all will change or perhaps disappear. By letting go of the labels, by letting go of me, my, mine, by looking at people, situations, and things, and accepting the temporary nature of their existence, we can reduce the worry, fear, anxiety, stress, and suffering we experience when they change or leave.

Perhaps it would be helpful to explore change and our relationship to it more closely, to better understand this concept of everything being empty. Change can be subtle. For example, your wife decides she wants short hair instead of long hair; but you really like her long hair. She's had long hair from the day you met, so when she cuts her hair you are disappointed because you were attached to her long hair. But that's really rather silly isn't it? After all, it's *her* hair, and hair grows back. Who knows, she may decide that she likes her long hair after all, but if the short hair makes her happy, then so what? Hair, because of its impermanent nature, is empty

Change can be dramatic. For example you are left paralyzed by an accident. Suddenly you can no longer do hundreds of things that, before the accident, you took for granted. Perhaps you need someone to help you perform even the simplest of activities like bathing or getting in and out of bed.   This is a significant change, but even in this example the principle of emptiness can be applied.   You were attached to your legs, you were attached to all the things that you could do with your legs.   You were attached to what having working legs represented.   However, does this mean your life is over? What can you still do, or what can you do instead?   Certainly letting go of our attachment is much more challenging here than in the first example, but in the end because they are impermanent, legs, like hair, are empty.

As I write this, our nation is beginning what is sure to be a long and heated debate over the issue of gun control; including what type and how many guns can one person have, how much and what type of ammunition can be purchased, and who should be prohibited from purchasing guns at all.   There is *tremendous* attachment to this issue along the entire continuum of possibilities.   One thing is certain; our attachment to guns and gun ownership (for or against) causes a great deal of suffering.   From the suffering of victims of gun violence, to the suffering caused by differing opinions on the issue, it is a classic example of what happens when we, as individuals, as well as a society, develop an intense attachment to an idea. In reality our impact on this issue, regardless of where we stand, will be a temporary one. The world that exists 100 years from now will be nothing like the world we live in today, anymore than the world that existed 100 years ago is like today's world.   It is only our attachment that fools us into thinking that what we do now will last forever. Ideology and laws, like legs and hair, are empty.

When we experience a loss, our illusion of permanence is shattered. The more dramatic and significant the loss, the greater our attachment, and therefore, the greater our suffering will be. However, if we can embrace the concept of emptiness, and cultivate a spirit of non- attachment, then we can reduce our suffering as changes occur.   You can begin to practice this on small, daily things; such as when you hit more red lights then you *expected* to hit on your drive to work, or you unexpectedly spill some coffee on your shirt.   Green lights and clean shirts

are temporary; after all, they too are empty.

As you master this concept with small things, you can

begin to apply it to larger ones.   For example, a family dispute

over how holidays *should* be celebrated.   Then you move on

to the tougher ones, like the loss of a beloved family pet.

Finally, we can apply the concept to the *really* big issues in life;

like divorce, financial ruin, or the death of a parent, spouse, or

child.   *All* of these things, conflicts, animals, relationships, and

people are going to change eventually.   *When* they change, as

well as the nature of the change, is unknown, but they *will*

change, and we will change as a result.   There will always be

pain, but we can reduce our suffering by releasing our

attachment to them.

Many people shy away from the idea that everything is

empty because they think it means a detachment of oneself

from society, relationships, love, and commitment.   In fact, it is

just the opposite.   Remember, not seeing the emptiness in

everything is what causes attachment. When we release ourselves from attachment, and the worry, fear, stress and anxiety that go with it we free ourselves to experiencing more compassion, more empathy, and deeper love because we are not caught up in our own suffering. In understanding emptiness, we see how the attachments that others have are causing them suffering, and we can extend compassion to them because we now know from where the root cause of their suffering emanates.

In a strange way, experiencing a significant loss accelerates this process because if we are to suvive, we must let go of our attachment to the person, relationship, or thing(s) that we lost. It's a bit of a crash course on the concept of emptiness. It is immersion in the profoundness of the law of impermanence. It is wisdom that once gained, is something we can share with others. We cannot eliminate pain from our lives or the lives of others, but we can reduce our suffering.

THE PITFALLS OF PLANNING

As I traveled the grief landscape, one of the most difficult things for me to let go of was the feeling that I should be accomplishing something.   I felt that I should be progressing along a certain path, that I should be feeling better, doing more, starting another business, planting a garden, or any number of other things.

I confess to being a serial planner.   I love making lists. Few things are more satisfying to me than the process of creating a list and then crossing items off the list as I complete them.   Setting goals and creating step by step action plans is one of my favorite ways to pass the time.   For many years these skills proved helpful when I was managing a department or setting up and growing my own business.

I tried very hard to plan my way out of grief after Don died.   My theory was that since these strategies had proven successful for me in the past it stood to reason that they would help me be successful in my recovery.   When you have no

reference for dealing with loss of that magnitude your natural

inclination is to go back to what you know.   So I made "to do"

lists, I set goals for myself, I wrote out and researched options

for where I might live, what type of work I might do, how I

would manage my money and even how often I would get out

of the house.   The problem was that I felt very little enthusiasm

for these plans.   It seemed pointless to plan for a future in

which I had no interest.   Furthermore, planning for things I

didn't care about didn't reduce my stress (as planning had done

for me in the past), but rather increased my level of stress and

anxiety.

It seemed that people were constantly asking me "what

are your plans?", and so naturally I felt like I ought to have

some.   I felt that by not having a plan, I was letting them (and

myself) down.   We live in a goal oriented world.   Work

performance appraisal systems, losing weight, getting fit;

everything you want or need to do in life comes with a

measurement system, a way to track your progress – yes Virginia, there's an "app" for that!   However well intentioned the "what are your plans?" question may be, for someone who has just experienced a loss, such questions are often counter-productive.   Some better questions to ask are: "What is important to you"? , "What are your priorities right now"? and "Is there anything I can do to help you figure things out"?

I allowed myself to get caught up in "having a plan". It ended up costing me. It cost me money, it cost me energy, and it cost me physically in terms of stress. I know now that it is perfectly okay to not always have a plan. I've learned how to let a day evolve on its own without a "to do" list.   I've learned that not always having a plan opens my life to opportunities that I would never have considered when I was in "implementing the plan" mode. I've learned when I *do* plan, to structure that plan more around what my values and priorities are, rather than focusing on just "getting something done". And I've learned that sometimes the best plan is having no plan.

The result is me being kinder and more patient with myself. When I'm expending my energy on being in the moment rather than thinking about what I may or may not be accomplishing I have less stress.

There are still times when I set goals and make lists, but I've gotten better at recognizing the difference between productive planning and non- productive planning.   Sometimes it's as simple as generating a "to do" list to motivate myself for the day when I'm feeling sluggish or blue. Sometimes its spending time reviewing or revising my "What Kind of Life Do I Want" exercise so I can see how a decision I'm about to make compares to the values and priorities I've identified for myself. However, when I start feeling overwhelmed or stressed during planning, that is a signal that I'm getting ahead of myself or thinking about going in a direction that it isn't right for me.

If you are recovering from a loss, you *will* need to make some decisions and do some planning. Your life is at a crossroads, either by choice or by fate.   Remember that it is okay to implement a temporary plan; one that will get you

through the crisis phase of your loss. When you are feeling less

raw and less emotional, *then* you can begin to think about what

your priorities and values are. This is what your decisions

should be based upon. Making a plan just for the sake of doing

something, or because others are pressuring you, is non-

productive planning, and you will likely end up with a less than

satisfactory result; or worse making a decision that you will

regret.

You don't need to achieve anything right now. You just

need to do the best that you can regardless of what our goal

obsessed culture wants you to believe.   Be kind to yourself

and let go of the expectations you or others may have for what

you should do and how you should feel. A wounded animal

expends all of its energy on recovering from injury.   When

dealing with a loss, we can apply nature's wisdom by following

nature's example.

WHAT IS IMPORTANT?

Loss brings suffering, but loss can also be a teacher. One of the unexpected "side effects" that I began to experience a couple of years after Don's death, was with regard to my emotional responses. I think this stemmed out of redefining what was important to me. As I observed the things in which the people around me (and the world in general) got caught up, I came to see how trivial most of it was. Many situations in our lives become elevated to the level of being important because of our emotional response to them. Deep down, we know they aren't *really* important, but we become so emotionally invested in them that their importance becomes inflated. For the purpose of this discussion, allow me to define those things that I think are most important.

- *Being alive is important*

- *Breathing is important*

- *Trying to do no harm is important*

- *Helping all living things achieve peace is important*

I realize this is a short list, but I think if all of our activities were related to these four simple points, we would be living a life that is focused on what is important. The first two points focus on the principle of being present in each moment. The last two are broader, and have to do with establishing values and priorities for how you want to live your life on a day to day basis, and how you want to interact with others. Once you define those values and priorities I think you will find that you spend less time in conflict, and more time in activities that bring clarity and meaning to your life.

We are creatures that live in a universe filled with opposites. Light and dark, hot and cold, rich and poor, black and white. We are habituated to think in these all or nothing terms. When it comes to emotional responses, there are three fundamental responses that create tension and conflict. I call them the *Three Poisons*. They are:

- *Greed*

- *Anger*

- *Ignorance*

Of course there are other options, for example, someone asked me why I didn't put "lust" on the poisons list. Lust is a form of greed, the first poison. Lust is the greed of feeling physical satisfaction, the greed to possess another person. The second poison, Anger, stems out of our need to be right about everything, to justify our actions, to defend ourselves against perceived wrongs. The third poison, Ignorance, is not about being stupid, it is about being stuck in a paradigm; restricting ourselves to a limited view of the world, or a certain viewpoint on an issue. These paradigms are often created as by-products of our upbringing, our religious beliefs, our prejudices, and perhaps most importantly, our fears.

The three poisons hold tremendous power in our lives. If we use them as a basis for how we react to people and situations, our lives become filled with tension and conflict. We quickly become sidetracked into believing that THESE are things that are important; my way, my opinion, my views, my belief, (what I call the "me, my, and mine" thinking).

Fortunately, there are antidotes to these poisons. They are:

- *Generosity*
- *Compassion*
- *Wisdom*

Generosity doesn't mean that you have to give all your money and belongings away, although most of us are capable of giving more than we think we can. Generosity is also about how we share our time – time to listen, time to assist, and time to be present for one another. The second antidote, Compassion, is the opposite of Anger because it means that we step back and feel empathy for another person's situation, their point of view. It means being non-judgmental. Compassion is not agreement and it is not acquiescence, it is simply having compassion for a fellow human being who is suffering; even when their suffering is affecting you.   The third antidote, Wisdom, is being willing to shift our own paradigms, to be open to other points of view, to not always needing to be right. Wisdom is also about knowing how to balance the first two antidotes; generosity and compassion.   There are times when we will need to be less generous with ourselves, for the sake of our health, and our own peace of mind.   There are times when we will need to speak truth in the face of obvious evil. While we may still feel compassion for the ones who are caught up in their own suffering because of the evil; we will need to speak for what is right and what is fair.   Sometimes, this kind of wisdom is applied on behalf of others, and sometimes we must apply this wisdom on behalf of ourselves.

However, if we approach life with the Three Antidotes in mind, if we use the antidotes as our "first line of defense", we are able to see more clearly the times it is necessary to protect ourselves.   Remember, what is truly important?

- *Being alive is important*

- *Breathing is important*

- *Trying to do no harm is important*

- *Helping all living things achieve peace is important*

There will always be some conflict and tension in our lives, but so much of it is because we *choose* for it to be there. We choose it by the people we associate with. We choose it by letting others define what is true for us rather than defining what is true for ourselves. We choose it by not being honest with ourselves, and then by default, not being honest with others. We choose it by the television programs we watch, the news we listen to, the websites we visit, the comments we post on-line. We choose it by what we put into our bodies. We choose it by being slaves to our own egos.

Think about all the areas of conflict in your life right now. Reread the previous paragraph. Did someone else create the conflict or tension, or did your own actions and reactions allow the conflict and tension to enter?

I read that some scientists now think the universe is contracting rather than expanding as was previously thought. Each of us is like a universe, since we are made up of the same molecules and sub atomic particles that make up every other thing in the universe. When we apply the Three Poisons as a way of interacting with the people in our lives and the planet we live on, we are functioning in the contracting universe theory. Our world implodes as it sinks under the weight of our greed, anger, and ignorance. On the other hand, when we apply the Three Antidotes as our model for interaction, we are functioning in the expanding universe theory. Imagine the ripples of energy we create when we use the 3 poisons. Our universe becomes smaller and smaller as we fold inward, suffocated by our stress, tension, and conflict. Now imagine those ripples of energy flowing outward when we use the 3 antidotes. Our universe expands as we practice generosity, compassion and wisdom.

And we are living our lives focused on what is important:

- *Being alive*

- *Breathing*

- *Doing no harm*

- *Helping all living things achieve peace*

As for me, I have a long way to go before I'm living fully in the expanding universe.   Most days it feels as though my ripples are swirling around in a mix of energy that is sometimes moving inward, sometimes moving outward; but by continuing to focus on what is important, and through practice, practice, practice, I think I can find my way.

HAPPINESS VERSUS PEACE

All living beings seek to be happy. The definition of happiness varies greatly between cultures, socio-economic levels, and even individuals. Here in the western world one could argue that we have become obsessed with finding happiness. We seek out partners, but when one or the other ceases "to be happy"; one partner leaves to seek out another. We seek comfortable dwellings, find one, fix it up, expand upon it, and change the landscaping only to decide that it is too old, too small, too "something" and move on to another one. We seek good food, good drink, good cars, good handbags and shoes. One only need look at television, magazines, talk radio, and bookstores to see how obsessed our culture is with finding happiness. We use credit cards and take out loans, all in the pursuit of happiness. We spend extravagant sums of money on creating the perfect wedding day, the perfect vacation, the perfect baby's room, the perfect party, because if we have everything "just so" we will be happy.

Certainly, there is nothing wrong with being happy, but what is happiness, really; and does it last?

This question of happiness is never more evident than when we lose something or someone that is precious to us. Happiness becomes an elusive entity and in our grief we are certain that we will never be happy again. I had such thoughts for several years after Don died. I felt that true happiness was beyond my grasp, I felt hopeless, and I would ask myself repeatedly: "Is this as good as it gets"? My life had become a boring routine. I found myself with no anticipation or enthusiasm for activities or events, and saw the future as a giant vacuum, filled only with worry and anxiety.

After joining my "Middle Path" Zen class, I began to reframe both my definition and expectation of happiness. I really considered these questions of "what is happiness," and "can one really be happy all of the time"? The answer to that second question is," of course not". The best we can hope for is to experience *moments* of happiness. For example, I remember how happy I was the day I got promoted to Vice President of Human Resources at a company I worked for. I was elated. I was an "executive". I got a nice big, juicy raise, and I was going to be eligible for big bonus dollars. Of course, along with the promotion came much more responsibility, longer hours at the office, and more sleepless nights. And while the job proved both challenging and rewarding, and while the company's owners treated me well, those feelings of euphoria and happiness I first experienced dissipated as the pressure of what the job required became real. Another example was my happiness when I bought my small house in my hometown. Don had been dead for nearly three years, and I thought a fresh start in a new home was a positive step in getting on with my life. It was closer to my job; and it had everything on my checklist; 2 bedrooms, 2 bathrooms, a garage, a small yard. I was elated. I moved in only to discover that every time we had a heavy rain, the basement leaked like a sieve. When it got really bad I had to spend hours sweeping and mopping up water. The basement, which I had hoped to use as an exercise and studio space was useless except for storage and even then, everything had to be packed in plastic and elevated. Needless to say, my happiness quickly turned to frustration. After two back-to-back heavy rainstorms and two sleepless nights spent in the basement trying to stay ahead of the water, I was finished with being a homeowner.

Happiness is fleeting. It is fleeting because it is an emotion and as with everything else, emotions are temporary. This is where we humans get into trouble, because we expect happiness to be our permanent state of existence. This is like expecting a bird to fly endlessly and never rest. It is like expecting every day to be sunny, but yet have no drought. It is an unreasonable expectation and impossible to attain.

So how then do we cope with the reality that happiness is fleeting? I believe there are two ways. The first is simply by acknowledging that all things are temporary, both the emotion and the state in which that emotion was created. By understanding and accepting this, it allows us to more fully appreciate the times when we do experience happiness; and to know that the more difficult emotions (pain, sorrow, loneliness) are equally temporary. The second way is to cultivate peace. Peace is not an emotion; peace is a state of being. We cannot always be happy, but we can always be at peace. Peace can be experienced even at the darkest and most frightening of times. Some people find peace through religion, by relinquishing their fate to a higher power. In Zen we cultivate peace by acknowledging the four noble truths: Life is suffering, suffering is caused by attachment, there is a way to alleviate suffering, and the way is to follow the 8 fold path. These are but two examples of methodologies that can achieve the same result. The first places the source of peace as coming from outside of oneself; the second places the source of peace as coming from inside of oneself. I am sure there are ways other than the two I have mentioned. I believe it is up to each of us, as seekers, to find our own path.

Personally, I choose to cultivate that peace from within myself - recognizing that it is my attachment to situations, emotions, people, places, and things that create my suffering. Acknowledging that all situations, emotions, people, places and things are impermanent, I can internalize the reality that nothing belongs to me, nothing is owed to me, nothing is guaranteed me, and in this realization, I can let go of my attachment to them.   When I accomplish this feat it is incredibly freeing, and I am left with a profound sense of peace. At first this practice really does feel like an accomplishment because it seems so difficult to do, and it is such a departure from our cultural way of thinking: "If only I was with so and so", "if only I got that job or that raise", "if only my parents, brothers, sisters weren't so difficult to deal with", "if only my boss wasn't such a jerk", "if only I could afford to eat out every week-end", "if only I were two sizes smaller", "if only I could take that cruise to the islands", if only, if only. All of these "if onlys" are really attachments and/or expectations.   These desires may come to pass, or they may not. You may have influence over them, or you may not. Certainly, it is okay for you to take steps to try and achieve your goals. Just remember you may not get the result you hope for; AND even if you do, that person is not always going to act the way you want them to, that job is not always going to be fun or rewarding, the weight may not stay off, and the money for that trip may have to be spent on something less glamorous. It's all temporary. Everything is fluid and in motion, changing all the time.

I liken change to water. Water, by its nature, is always changing. I love living by the water, especially large bodies of water, but any water will do. Sometimes water is calm and smooth, what kayakers call "flat water". Sometimes it is rough and boisterous. Sometimes it is running strong and fast, as a stream after rainfall. Sometimes it is a soft babbling brook. Sometimes it is frozen as a pond during winter. Sometimes it is a barely a trickle, as in times of drought. Water is always water, but it is never the same.

So it is with happiness.   With the impermanent nature

of the fabric of life, we must let go of the expectation that we

will always be happy.   You say, "Well I know that I can't always

be happy". But do you, really? If that is so then why do you

(and I) expend so much effort trying to get back to "being

happy" when we are not?   A much better use of our energy

would be to cultivate peace, for we can always return to that

place of peace no matter what our external circumstances are.

As my year in Maine was coming to a close, I had an

opportunity to meet Sunim, a Buddhist monk, from Korea. A

few months earlier he had decided to leave his monastery in

Korea and bicycle across North and South America. He knew

only one or two people, his English was limited, and his Spanish

even more limited. He had only enough money to buy a second

hand bike, and not one that was really designed for long

distance travel. He bought meager camping equipment. He

had only walking sandals and a lightweight jacket.   He

expected to be traveling for at least two years. He felt that he needed to take on this challenge to really live his philosophies

and enhance his own practice of Zen Buddhism. He was 42

years old and had spent his entire adult life in the monastery.

His route happened to take him through Maine after he

had biked across Canada. Through a series of remarkable

events he was rarely having to camp, and had a network of

people who were working to secure warm showers,

comfortable beds, and healthy meals for him along the way. He

spent a weekend at the home of the woman who had

established the local Zen Buddhist center I attended. She and

her husband, and another couple from our center, hosted a

dinner in Sunim's honor while he was in our area. Even during

the few hours that I spent in his company it was clear that he

was someone who really understood the concepts of

impermanence and being present in the here and now. He took

each day as it came. He was totally with whomever he was

with; giving them his full attention and not thinking or worrying

about the people he was going to be with tomorrow. He

accepted what was given him. For example, on this trip even though he was a vegetarian, he ate the meat dishes placed before him (as not all of his hosts realized he was a vegetarian) with an attitude of gratefulness. He accepted that sometimes he would be tired, and in pain. He accepted that some days he would be riding in bad weather and that he might have to sleep on the ground. He accepted that some days would be glorious and he would get to see beautiful scenery and bustling cities. His gratitude, humility and compassion were evident in his demeanor and his actions. So was his peace. One of the most beautiful things about his journey was not only what it was teaching him, but what it was teaching the hundreds of people he met along the way; an outcome he certainly could not have imagined when he embarked upon his journey.

We are not all so fortunate to have years to spend cultivating and practicing the principles of Zen Buddhism. But we can learn from Sunim's example and apply these principles in small doses each day that we have. We can do it by recognizing when we are attached to a particular outcome; the outcome we think will bring us happiness. We can do it by being grateful for the people and places and *moments* of happiness we experience. Treasure them, for they are fleeting. We can do it by reminding ourselves that being uncomfortable is part of the human experience. We can do it by sitting quietly and breathing. We can do it by appreciating a child's smile, a sunset, a snowflake, a hug.

This idea of happiness versus peace is an ongoing practice for me. It isn't something that you "get" and then you have it. You "get" the concept, but then you work at it moment by moment, day by day. I guess that is why they call it practice.

Whatever your circumstances, I DO wish you happiness, but most of all, I wish you peace.

RECOVERY DEFINED

Many of the books I read about grieving and the "process" of grieving had these wonderful happy endings. The grieving person took tragedy and turned it into something meaningful. They took their anger and grief and started, or got involved in, a cause related to their loss. They started charities to honor their loved ones. They ran a marathon. They fell in love again and reclaimed happiness. The books that didn't conclude with happy endings had instead a process. They had "steps" or "stages", and if you and I, as grievers, would only follow these steps or stages, then we too would have a happy ending. Invariably, these "step" books were accompanied by acronyms like S.O.A.R, or T.R.A.N.S.C.E.N.D.. The "step" books were often written by "experts", therapists, counselors; all well intentioned people to be sure, but few of them had yet to go through a life altering loss. The "happy ending" books were generally written by survivors of loss. I understand that in life, as in fiction, we want happy endings. We want hope, and we want to believe that there can be a happy ending for us too.

I'm glad these authors found happy endings or found a way to turn their loss into something positive. The reality is that, for most of us, the ending is not so dramatic. There is no knight in shining armor, no NPO, (non- profit organization), no marathons, no acronyms. Recovery for most of us is much more subtle, much less dramatic; a baby's smile, a home in a different city, or a new hobby. It is learning to live alone, learning to live with less, learning to live without the illusions of control and security. It is passing through fire and learning to live with the scars. It is redefining our faith or letting it go. It rarely has an "end" point. Surviving our loss is more like a backpack we carry with us on the journey. The only question is how heavy are we going to make that backpack and how much weight do we want to carry with us?

Sorry to disappoint you, but this book isn't going to end with a traditional happy ending. As I write this, my life is far from the way I would like it to be.   On most days I still feel that I would be happier and more content if Don was alive and we were together.   If string theory turns out to be real, then perhaps in some alternate universe we are together, and that's a comforting thought.   However, in *this* universe, in *this* time and space I continue to recover.   I don't know at what point I will say that I am "recovered", for as I said, I'm not sure there is an end point to this journey.   But I have been able to lighten my backpack by how I integrate the things that have happened to me into my daily existence.   Some losses I am able to integrate more quickly and they don't alter my path's trajectory.   Other losses, like the loss of Don, have taken much longer for me to integrate and have altered my trajectory considerably.

Loss presents us with a "koan".   In Zen practice koans are given to the student by their teacher as a way to strengthen their meditative practice or deepen their enlightenment.   They are like riddles, and there is no one right answer.   Rather it is about finding the right answer for that particular student and what he or she needs to learn or understand at that point in time.   So it is with the koan called "loss".   It comes to us not because we ask for it, but because it must come.   It is a universal riddle, a part of the human condition.   What you take from your loss experience and how you answer your loss riddle or koan is going to be different from what I take from mine. There is no right or wrong answer. However, if we have any interest in enhancing our human experience, we should try and use our losses as a way to deepen our understanding of this journey we call "life".   Pain, whether it is physical, emotional, or spiritual is a great teacher.

As I grappled with my own loss koan I listened to a lot of music.   There were a number of songs that I found especially meaningful.   Some of them resonated with me in just a phrase, others with a chorus or a verse.   Some of the songs were new to me, others were songs I had listened to most of my life, but they took on a new meaning for me as I traversed the grief landscape.

There is one song in particular that I listened to many times while thinking about this chapter. That is "Thank U" by Alanis Morriset. In it she presents us with a "koan", a beautiful metaphor for recovery from loss.

"The moment I let go of it, was the moment I got more than I could handle. The moment I jumped off of it, was the moment I touched down"

For me these lyrics are saying that recovery from loss is not a linear process, it is not a neat series of steps or stages. What we expect to have happen is not always what we get.

Living with a spirit of gratitude and humbleness, in the face of unbearable pain, is perhaps the best definition of "recovery" that I can give you. It is asking questions and sometimes hearing nothing but silence in return. It is letting go of our illusions. It is expanding our vision to see the entire quilt of life, not just our own small square. It is recognizing that sometimes when we feel the weakest, we are most strong.

This recovery is yours. It is not mine. How you define it, how you integrate your loss into your life's fabric will be

231

different from how I define and integrate mine. What is common to all of us is the loss. What we can share is compassion; compassion for ourselves and compassion for others.

MOMENTS OF PANIC, MOMENTS OF PEACE

I sit here in the midst of a raging category one Hurricane (my first), also known as the Super Storm "Sandy" and I am strangely at peace. I arrived at this location along the Chesapeake Bay less than 48 hours earlier to rent this house for the winter and write this book.

What a departure from a few years ago, when I didn't feel capable of handling anything close to this. The fact was, then, it was less about my <u>ability</u> to handle things as much as it was my <u>resistance</u> to handling things. For a long time I resented being forced to deal with issues and problems by myself. Certainly at first, after the shock and loss of Don, my ability to handle stress was diminished. But as time went on, and I regained strength, it became a deep seeded resentment that handling problems, making large and small decisions alone was something I was forced to do, rather than something I had chosen to do. That just didn't sit well with me. So, when challenges arose I would grumble and moan and lament (mostly to myself) about the unfairness of the situation, rather than doing what needed to be done and moving on.

Now, living in a location five feet above sea level, less than 100 yards away from the water, during a storm, I feel like I'm okay. It isn't glib "live in the moment" thinking; I have done my research (looking at flood plain maps on line, getting feedback from neighbors), I have laid in supplies (I'm writing this in the dark without power by the way), and I have signed up with the county EMS notification system.

I've allowed myself to flow through the panic. I eyed the water level in the marina across the street, CERTAIN that it was going to overflow and I would be climbing to the 2nd floor of my new home. The news, which I watched nonstop before the cable went out, tries to help by providing "information"; but mostly I find that they only serve to increase the panic. It is the law of diminishing returns – the more "information" they put out, the less it resembles information and the more it becomes about building fear.

The power has gone out and it is dark- beyond dark. I can no longer see the marina. When is high tide? How high is the water now?   So easy to give into fear.

Stop, wait. WHAT IS TRUE?   This valuable question learned months ago in a "Middle Path" Zen class comes back to me. What IS true? It is true that it is VERY windy. It is true that there is a copious amount of rain falling from the sky. It is true that the power is out, that the phone and internet are out. It is true that the water is rising, but the authorities and people who have lived here for years don't think it will cause dangerous flooding.

It is also true that trucks are routinely driving up and down my street, volunteer fire personnel out in this awful weather checking on things. It is also true that marina employees are taking shifts, riding out the storm in the marina building; I see the cars change every few hours.

Am I alone?   Aloneness is, for most of us (unless you are living in the wilderness), a state of mind. Obviously there are people nearby. I can look up and down the street and see the glow of candles. I know from the vehicles I have seen that there are other people nearby.   This storm will pass. The power outage, the lack of communication tools (phone, internet) will all get all turned on again.

I can attach to the panic or I can accept the peace.   I light my first wood fire; it takes the chill off the house. My hurricane lantern glows softly, as do the flickering votive candles throughout the house. The storm is a reminder that I am in charge of NOTHING except my own actions and reactions. I have opened one of the windows a crack to let some of the excess heat of my fire escape.   The wind continues to howl, but it no longer creates panic. Rather it seems like an old friend reminding me that ALL things are fleeting, for indeed this storm is in the process of passing.

I heard weather forecasters describing this as "the Perfect Storm". Perhaps this WAS the perfect storm, at the perfect time to propel me into this next stage of my life.

Panic or peace. We make the choice moment by moment. Panic will come, it is inevitable, and it is part of being human. Choose to attach to panic and it will drain you of energy and of self confidence. Panic doesn't have to be an out and out stampede (as depicted in disaster movies). Panic can be insidious, like little pins pricking away at us – "be afraid, be afraid, be afraid", "you can't handle this", "you don't know what will happen", and so on and so on the inner dialogue goes until panic is the only voice we hear.

Attach to the panic or accept the peace. When the panic comes ask yourself: "What is true"? What do you know FOR CERTAIN about this particular moment? When you have answered that question then ask yourself: "How can I react to what is true"? Does reacting with panic make the situation any better? Does it EVER help you feel more in control? Does it build you up or tear you down? Does it make you feel strong or does it make you feel weak? Nine times out of ten we attach to feelings of panic because we lack information, or we can't see or know what is going to happen next. Remember that the "next moment" may never come; or what is more likely, the "next moment" is not going to look anything like the one you imagined. So why waste time and energy on it? There will be storms in our lives, and some will feel like a Category Five hurricane, but even the strongest storms are temporary. When we attach to the panic we feed it, and in doing so, allow it to linger longer and be more devastating than it needs to be.

Accept the peace.   Accept that in this moment you may not have all the information you would like to have. Accept that in this moment you don't know what is going to happen next, and that's okay; because when the next moment comes, you will be in it continuing to accept the peace. Accept that each moment is temporary, flowing and moving us from one place to the next.   Moments of panic or moments of

peace? Accept the peace.

ACKNOWLEDGMENTS

No one finds their way out of loss alone, and no author writes a book alone. I would like to take *this* moment to gratefully acknowledge the help and support (wittingly or unwittingly) of the following:

To the family and friends who sat with me, cried with me, and cared for me in the days, weeks and months after Don's death, your names are too numerous to mention. Thanks also to my family for your moral and emotional support of my sudden decision to move to Maine. To my "adopted" "family" in Maine, who embraced my quest and encouraged me to "keep walking". To Reverand Laura Bonyon-Neal and the folks at Cattitudes, and the True Nature Zen Center; thank you for giving me a "safe" place to explore the concepts of Zen as they relate to life and loss. To my "beta readers"; Linda Brenneman, Norm Yunginger, Phyllis Dietz, Todd Smith, and Laura Neal – your feedback, corrections, and suggestions have given me a more polished manuscript and a better book. To Barb Carper, friend extraordinaire, thank you for driving up and down the eastern seaboard with me, for keeping me "on task" with writing this book, for being my "alpha reader", and all around good egg; your support and enthusiasm for my journey is much appreciated. To the many readers of my blog "Acadian Soul" who faithfully followed my adventures in Maine, and later in Maryland. And finally, to Acadia National Park – not a person, but a place; thank you for your views and your vistas, for your quiet roads and your challenging trails; thank you for just being "there", not just for me, but for anyone seeking peace and restoration.

ABOUT THE AUTHOR

Carol Potter was born and raised in south central Pennsylvania. After the sudden death of her husband in 2007, she moved to a small coastal town in "Down East" Maine, and later lived along the Chesapeake Bay (where this book was written). Her passions are walking, photography, Acadia National Park, and the company of good friends and family. She currently resides in Lancaster, Pennsylvania with her two furry companions: Pebbles and Bam Bam. This is her first book.